Constitutional Issues in Correctional Administration

Constitutional Issues in Correctional Administration

Chadwick L. Shook
Robert T. Sigler

Carolina Academic Press / Durham, North Carolina

ISBN 0-89089-936-3
LCCN 00-102932

Carolina Academic Press
700 Kent Street
Durham, North Carolina 27705
Telephone (919) 489-7486
Fax (919) 493-5668
E-mail: cap@cap-press.com
www.cap-press.com

Printed in the United States of America.

To My Parents: Thank you for all your love, support, and encouragement... I love you.

CLS

Contents

Table of Cases

TABLE OF CASES XIII

About the Authors:

Chadwick L. Shook

Chad Shook serves as judicial law clerk to the Honorable Mary Libby Payne of the Court of Appeals of Mississippi. He holds the Doctorate of Jurisprudence from the Mississippi College School of Law and a Masters of Science in Criminal Justice from the University of Alabama. Aside from his interest in institutional corrections, Chad's other areas of interest include substantive and procedural criminal law, constitutional law, and judicial process. Chad is member of the Academy of Criminal Justice Sciences, the Southern Criminal Justice Association, the American Correctional Association, and the American Bar Association. Chad is licensed to practice law in Alabama, Georgia, and Mississippi. Effective July 10, 2000, Chad will associate with the law firm of Upshaw, Williams, Biggers, Beckham, & Riddick in Greenwood, Mississippi.

Robert T. Sigler

Bob Sigler is a professor in the Department of Criminal Justice at the University of Alabama. In addition to his interest in corrections, Bob conducts research on and has published in the areas of domestic violence and courtship violence (with an emphasis on forced sexual intercourse) with Dr. Ida Johnson, the criminalization of domestic violence (also with Dr. Ida Johnson) and stress in justice system employees. He presently serves on ALERT, a committee of the Alabama Department of Corrections which is tasked with developing an effective plan for the management of facilities that house and treat women sentenced to the Department's custody. As a part of his committee responsibilities he is conducting a study of women sentenced to life without parole with Dr. Etta Morgan. A companion book written with Greg Vecchi focuses on criminal and civil forfeiture.

Constitutional Issues in Correctional Administration

Introduction

Few issues have received the attention in the past two decades that has been characteristic of the on going debate about inmate rights. Historically, inmates had no rights. Once some one was judged to have violated the laws of society sufficiently to warrant incarceration, he or she was held to have forfeited the rights that were due to the law abiding citizens of his or her country. During the twentieth century, Western society matured to the point that individual rights, particularly the rights of relatively defenseless individuals such as children, women, and the mentally ill, were championed by active social reformers from the middle and upper classes. While inmates were the last disenfranchised group to be championed, the 1950s and 1960s saw increasing attention to the rights of those incarcerated for failure to conform to the values accepted by law abiding citizens.

Two systems that were particularly troubling provided a foothold for the reformers. The problems in the administration of the prisons in Alabama and Arkansas were sufficiently severe that ordinary men and women of good conscience could not condone the manner of operation of these prisons. The litigation that was produced overturned the hands-off doctrine, led to the declaration of those two systems as unconstitutional in the totality of their operations, and opened the gate for challenges from inmate advocates in other states. Alabama and Arkansas reformed their systems and by the 1970s were operating well managed systems that were sensitive to the rights and needs of the inmates they held. Other prison and jail systems moved to conform to the standards for operation established by the courts.

Litigation for inmates' rights, once unleashed, was not reduced by the compliance of correctional managers. The floodgates were open and the courts became inundated in suits filed by inmates or their advocates challenging every perceived violation of rights in the operation of the prison. While a number of areas appear to be settled with the enunciation of clear standards that strike a balance between inmate rights and the needs of the managers to operate safe and secure institutions, other areas continue to be litigated. This book seeks to review both those areas that appear to be settled and those areas in which the issues to be litigated are still open to interpretation.

Inmate access to the courts continues to be litigated and is addressed in two chapters. The courts continue to support the contention that access to the courts is a right that is retained by inmates. This right is not absolute in that inmates do not have the right to pursue frivolous suits or to have access to legal resources in an attempt to find a legally actionable issue. Courts, which hear challenges to institutional practices, must recognize the needs of correctional managers to maintain an efficient operation and a safe environment. While access is assured, no single set of resources or any specific approach to assuring access is mandated. Legislation reducing the flow of frivolous suits has been affirmed and many states are developing strategies to reduce the flow of frivolous complaints without violating the inmates' right to access to the courts.

Freedom of religion has continued to provide litigation but is more settled than other areas due primarily to the intervention of Congress. The passage of the Religious Freedom Restoration Act of 1993 placed an affirmative but ineffective burden on correctional administrators. Restrictions on the freedom of expression of religion are still possible if the exercise of those rights constitute a demonstrable threat to the effective management of the institution but the least restrictive alternative consistent with institutional safety must be adopted.

Prison overcrowding is reemerging as a critical factor in correctional administration. Much of the growth in prison populations can be attributed to a change in societal orientation toward the disposition of criminal offenders. Two schools of thought dominate sentencing philosophies, the classical school and the positive school. The positive school focuses on the offender and produces a rehabilitative emphasis in sentencing. The classical school focuses on the crime and deterrence but usually produces punitive sentences. Society cycles between two extremes based on these two different philosophies. At present the classical perspective is dominant and legislatures are producing statutes which require that offenders serve their full sentences, place habitual offenders in prison for the rest of their lives, and enhances existing sentences for a number of reasons. The result is a rapidly growing prison population with relatively little additional financial support.

Capital punishment continues to be an issue and can be expected to produce litigation into the foreseeable future. Housing death row inmates places additional burdens on correctional managers. The Supreme Court has held that the death penalty is not per se cruel and unusual if it is not discriminatorily applied. The cruel and unusual nature of the form of execution has been challenged and remains unsettled. Issues regarding conditions of death row cells was challenged in many of the original cases brought before the court challenging the hands-off doctrine. It is likely that litigation will focus on these conditions at some time in the future.

The issue of privatization was settled in the 1930s when organized labor joined with business to protest the use of prison labor to compete on the open market. All states and the federal government moved to a state use system and the use of prison labor by private businesses ended. The privatization issue has reemerged in a different form. The use of prison labor in the private sector is wide spread but is not generating opposition from labor and business. This is due, in part, to the prevailing wage provisions in enabling statutes which prevents prison labor from competing unfairly with private labor. The new issues are related to the privatization of prison management. The issue of liability and immunity dominate the litigation to this point with private contractors denied the limited immunity available to state employees.

The standard of medical care due an inmate produced extensive litigation from the first cases brought before the courts. Adequate medical treatment is a right that confers a duty to correctional administrators. While the level of care need not be exceptional, normal or standard care must be delivered. Challenges to the level of medical care provided or denied produced the deliberate indifference standard that has come to be broadly applied.

Control of the institution underlies much of the controversy in specific areas such as religion and medical care. Correctional staff are thinly spread and are compelled to emphasize inmate control to maintain a safe and secure environment. Inmates seek to gain as much control over their environment as possible. The courts have generally supported correctional officials when inmates contest restricted movement, searches of persons and property, or contact with the outside world as long as the rules challenged meet legitimate institutional needs and are not capricious in their application.

In the coming chapters we will examine each of these areas in depth. Both historical antecedents and contemporary activity will be presented to allow the reader both to place the issues in context and to assess where we stand today.

Chapter 1

The Evolution of Prisoners' Rights

The status of inmates in prisons in the United States has varied considerably as the administration of prisons has evolved. The first prisons were dedicated to rehabilitation; thus, inmates' rights were not an issue. Early prison philosophy held that inmates lost all status in society and could be treated or housed in any manner that the keepers felt desirable or economically feasible. Early civil death statutes that stripped inmates of all civil rights expressed this orientation. This philosophy was reflected in the decisions in cases brought before the Supreme Court which articulated the position which came to be identified as the hands-off doctrine. Before redefinition of responsibilities of departments of corrections in the 1960s, prison inmates had few rights. States were permitted to operate their prisons as they saw fit. Most states denied inmates the right to complain about the nature of their incarceration and conveyed considerable discretion to wardens in the nature of prison operations and the application of discipline in prisons. Attempts by inmates and advocates of prison reform to force wardens and commissioners of corrections to change the manner in which they operated their prisons by seeking legal redress were unsuccessful at the state level.

Attempts to invoke federal intervention by inmates and their advocates were systematically denied under the well-established hands-off doctrine. The hands-off doctrine held that the federal government had no legal standing to interfere in the operations of state institutions. Inmate advocate groups exposed extreme sub-standard conditions in many prisons in the United States. They were successful in changing public sentiment that provided the impetus needed to breach the hands-off doctrine in the 1960s. Once the doctrine was breached by cases documenting these unacceptable conditions, federal intervention rapidly expanded to address a full range of inmates' rights. Today, the basis for intervention by the federal courts in the operation of state institutions can be found in a number of constitutional issues and legislative initiatives. This chapter examines the initial breach of the hands-off doctrine and the subsequent expansion of inmate rights. Subsequent chapters will address areas that continue to be actively litigated by inmates and their advocates.

Establishing the Doctrine

The principle of the hands-off doctrine was first enunciated in *Pervear v. Massachusetts* (1866). The inmate plaintiff argued that prison conditions in and of themselves in Massachusetts violated the cruel and unusual punishment clause of the Eighth Amendment. The court held that the federal government had no legitimate interest in the operation of state institutions and that the Eighth Amendment protections were not applicable to inmates in state prisons.

A second case, *Ruffin v. Commonwealth* (1871), declared that inmates in Virginia did not have the right to judicial review of complaints regarding their incarceration; inmates were declared "slaves of the state." As such inmates did not have standing as citizens and forfeited all of their rights when sentenced to prison. This issue did not rise again until 1941 when a challenge to denial of access to the courts was heard by the United States Supreme Court. The Court in *Ex Parte Hull* (1941) held that while inmates did have a right to judicial review, relief was not justified by the facts in the case presented to the court, and the hands-off doctrine continued in force. The hands-off doctrine continued to be held as established doctrine in a decision rendered in *Coffin v. Reichard* (1944) in which the issue focused more clearly on conditions within an institution. As late as 1958, the United States Supreme Court affirmed the long-standing non-intervention doctrine in *Gore v. United States* (1958).

Breaking the Hands-Off Doctrine

In 1964, the hands-off doctrine was challenged in principle in *Cooper v. Pate* (1964) when the Supreme Court held that prisoners had the right to have grievances addressed under the Civil Rights Act of 1871. While not a constitutional issue, the *Cooper* decision provided the first basis for the breaching of the hands-off doctrine. This decision was followed by a series of cases dealing with prison conditions in two states, Alabama and Arkansas, that effectively displaced the hands-off doctrine.

In Arkansas, a series of decisions beginning in 1965 and extending through 1969 challenged specific aspects of the operation of the Arkansas prison system as violating protections offered to all people in the United States by the Eighth Amendment. The first decisions, which recognized that prison inmates retain some of the rights afforded under the constitution, focused on disciplinary procedures. The hands-off doctrine was first breached in *Talley v. Stevens* (1965). The court ruled that standardless corporal punishment administered to prison inmates violated the Cruel and Unusual Punishment Clause of the Eighth Amendment. Under the decision, corporal punishment in Arkansas was suspended until clear standards for determining the validity of accusations and for determining appropriate administrative sanctions for inmate misbehavior by department of corrections personnel were developed. Two subsequent decisions, *Jackson v. Bishop* (1968) and *Holt ·v. Sarver* (1969), modified this order reinforcing the breach of the hands-off doctrine in the process. The rulings in *Talley v. Stevens* and *Jackson v. Bishop* were expanded to include basic living conditions in *Holt v. Sarver II* (1969), and in 1970 the operation of the Arkansas prison system

in and of itself was held to be in violation of the cruel and unusual punishment provisions of the Eighth Amendment.

Alabama was the second state that the federal district court
found to be in violation of the Eighth Amendment in the totality
of its operations. The first complaint alleged that inmates held in
Alabama prisons were denied effective medical care and that this
denial violated the cruel and unusual provisions of the Eighth
Amendment. In 1972, the federal court held that depravation of
basic medical care in Alabama institutions for prisoners was a violation of the Eighth Amendment (*Newman v. Alabama*, 1972).
This decision was followed in 1976 by litigation asserting that
the operation of the prison system in its totality was a violation of
the Eighth Amendment (*Pugh v. Locke*, 1976). The court found
for the plaintiffs and ordered comprehensive reform in the operation of institutions managed by the Alabama Department of
Corrections.

The hands-off doctrine was not simply challenged or diminished; it was displaced by the affirmative imposition of standards,
which federal judges deemed to meet constitutional requirements,
by court order. In this series of decisions in cases brought against
the prison systems in these two states, sweeping orders were issued
which set specific conditions and standards for operation of the
prison system and established oversight commissions which re-
ported directly to the federal courts. While some of these decisions rendered by federal district courts were appealed by the departments of correction which were being challenged, the circuit
courts of appeal generally supported the concepts expressed by
the lower courts. Remands or partial reversals focused on the specific court order and not on the challenge to the principles underlying the hands-off doctrine. The first state department of corrections to strongly resist the breach of the hands-off doctrine was
Texas; however, by 1980 the reversal of the hands-off doctrine was
well established and the decisions of the district courts issuing orders regulating the Texas Department of Corrections were upheld.

Two sets of factors that influenced the court as it deliberated
its decisions were in operation at the time of the breach of the

hands-off doctrine and may have produced the challenges to the full loss of rights conferred by the federal constitution by state managed inmates implied in the hands-off doctrine. First, during the 1960s and 1970s, inmate rights oriented reform activists challenged the operations of U.S. prisons from coast to coast. State based coalitions promoted inmate rights documenting harsh disciplinary measures and deteriorating living conditions in America's aging and poorly supported correctional institutions. Second, extreme conditions existing in some prisons were so severe that they could not withstand pubic scrutiny in even the most conservative social settings. To some extent it can be argued that the federal judicial system was used to force state legislatures to allocate adequate resources to the operation of state prison systems (Smollo, 1984). This assertion has been challenged by Montick (1983) who stated that judicial intervention is not sufficient to deal with a problem that is caused by inadequate budgets provided by apathetic legislatures. It should be noted that in the three states that provided the majority of the cases that set the stage for the breach of the hands-off doctrine, inadequate resources appear to be a key contributor to the conditions which justified federal intervention.

At the time of the successful challenge of the conditions and management strategies characteristic of the Arkansas prison system, prison conditions in that state were severe. The Arkansas prison system was managed by a very small core of paid employees who were administrators. All of the guards were inmates. Inmate shotgun guards guarded the common inmates and inmate rifle guards guarded the shotgun guards. These conditions created an environment in which protection, medical services, food, and all other resources were controlled by inmates who advanced their positions though the use of extortion and intimidation. The resources that were made available by the prison system were inadequate for the maintenance of personal physical and mental health and the inmate guards were capricious and cruel in the administration of "discipline." The operation of the Arkansas prison system during the years before the breach of the hands-off doctrine so violated the basic rights of inmates that its operation could not be defended. Tom Murton, the former superintendent of the Arkansas prison system, and Joe Hyams co-authored *Accomplices to the Crime* (1969) which provides details of the prison conditions and the politics that controlled the Arkansas prison system and which hindered the development of a professional Arkansas Department of Corrections. Arkansas Governor Winthrop Rockefeller realized that the state prison system needed a major overhaul and began to institute reform; however, he was met with hostility from the legislature and an unsympathetic electorate. Murton and Hyams (1969) relate that discipline was maintained by the use of inhumane techniques including electric shocks that were also used as a means to get information from inmates. Tom Murton became superintendent in February 1967 and served in this capacity until March 1968. Murton's departure was proceeded two months by his discovery of three skeletons, which he suspected were murdered inmates, on the grounds of the Cummins Farm prison.

The conditions in the institutions of the Arkansas prison system were completely unacceptable by any standard; thus, imposition of federal standards was a reasonable response. As noted above, the governor of Arkansas had embarked on a program of prison reform before these cases were brought, but reform efforts were meeting resistance from elements in the community who profited financially from the operation of the extensive farming component of the prison system operations and from members of the legislature who preferred to preserve the income producing function of the prison system. The large farming operation produced an income which more than covered the budget allocation for the operation of the system.

Similar but less severe conditions existed in the Alabama Department of Corrections. The deterioration of the Alabama system can be attributed in part to reform efforts and in part to the failure of the governor and the legislature to provide adequate resources to operate the prison system. In the 1960s, the Alabama Department of Corrections closed old Kilby Prison and the physical plant was removed. Old Kilby was a large prison that was difficult to manage and which was in advanced stages of decay. The approximately 1,000 beds which were lost were not immediately replaced causing severe overcrowding which was aggravated by subsequent "get-tough" legislation increasing the use of incarceration as a sanction. The governor resisted all attempts to produce legislation to increase support for the state's prisons. Severe overcrowding and lack of financial support from the legislature and continued deterioration of relatively old over-burdened physical plants produced severe living conditions which were easy to challenge and difficult to defend.

Deterioration in the institutions of the Texas Department of Corrections in the late 1970s was less severe than was the case in Alabama but the breach of the standard was well established at the district court level by the time that cases challenging the operation of Texas prisons were brought. Texas experienced rapid growth in inmate population and in prison construction that was not matched with a corresponding growth in operating budget, particularly in staffing. Control of the prison population was maintained through the use of a prison tender system in which inmates guarded inmates. As the staff/inmate ratio deteriorated, the power of inmate tenders increased. The result was an increase in extortion and abuse of power similar though less severe to that observed in the Arkansas system. Documented cases of persistent severe abuse were difficult to defend and warranted substantial federal intervention.

The action of organized prison reform groups combined with instances of extreme conditions in selected prisons led to the breach of the hands-off doctrine and the application of the cruel and unusual punishment provisions of the Eighth Amendment to the operation of several prison systems. In Alabama, the intervention of the federal courts was exceptionally specific and detailed. Defects cited in the Alabama system included the failure of the state to provide basic items for personal hygiene such as toothpaste, toothbrushes, shampoo, and combs; conditions produced by the deteriorating physical plants such as exposed wiring, inadequate plumbing, and inadequate heating; poor nutrition in both planning and delivery of meals; absence of treatment and rehabilitation programs; and the inadequate application of a classification process. Inadequate funding by the state legislature was held to be an inadequate defense. The United States District Court for the Middle District of Alabama, under the pen of the late Judge Frank Johnson, Jr., appointed a human rights council to oversee the operation of the prisons and to set minimum constitutional standards for operating correctional institutions including a minimum of 40 square feet of living space for each inmate, a limit of 21 days on the use of isolation, a minimum of 30 minutes of exercise per inmate per day, reading and writing materials for each inmate (including those in isolation), and minimum staffing levels for each of the institutions in the state (*Pugh v. Locke*, 1976).

Once the doctrine was breached, cases rising from less severe conditions moved forward. The hands-off doctrine was replaced by the "deliberate indifference" standard. The deliberate indifference standard was first enunciated in a case in which the plaintiff-inmate claimed inadequate medical care inside the institution. The United States Supreme Court held that in order to prevail, the plaintiff would need to establish that the state officials had demonstrated a deliberate indifference to his needs and that in the case under review, this standard had not been met (*Estelle v. Gamble*, 1976). The deliberate indifference standard established in *Estelle* was extended to all aspects of prison confinement in 1991 when the court held that establishing the state of mind of 22 prison officials was a key factor in the determination that the action of the officials constituted a violation of the cruel and unusual provisions of the Eighth Amendment (*Wilson v. Seiter*, 1991). This position was reinforced in *Farmer v. Brennan* (1994).

Cases were heard addressing or clarifying issues such as the degree of force that can be used to control disruptive inmates. The Supreme Court has generally approved of the use of reasonable physical force administered by correctional officers to maintain order behind prison walls unless the use of force is applied with the deliberate intent to cause injury and if the force is not related to the officer's responsibility to maintain order (*Martinez v. Rosado*, 1979). Palmer (1991) noted that this decision did not protect correctional administrators from civil and constitutional suits when the use of force was unreasonable. In *Hudson v. McMillian* (1992), the Supreme Court moderated the deliberate indifference standard in cases involving the use of force by holding that the use of excessive force may violate inmates' rights regardless of the extent of injuries or the situation in which the force is used. Mohs (1993) suggested that this decision would create serious difficulties for prison administrators, and Butler (1993) suggested that the outcome would be a flood of new cases based on the cruel and unusual punishment provision of the Eighth Amendment but that the use of unjustified force in prisons would decline.

Sources of Federal Challenges to the Operation of State Institutions

Prison inmates and their advocates have continued to challenge the methods employed by state officials in the management of state correctional facilities. These challenges have emerged from a number of legal perspectives and have tended to be very broad. Actions have been brought alleging violations of the United States Constitution and violations of a range of federal statutes.

Constitutional Challenges

Constitutional challenges have alleged violations of protections afforded by a number of amendments that have been added to the Constitution to protect individual rights. Challenges include cases brought forward regarding the First, Fourth, Eighth, and Fourteenth Amendments. While challenges are often brought which allege violation of more that one constitutional standard, decisions will be addressed in this section that appear to have provided the primary rational for the decision.

First Amendment Challenges. The First Amendment protects freedom of religion, freedom of association, freedom of speech, and freedom to assemble peacefully. Most suits alleging first amendment violations brought forward by inmates have addressed freedom of speech and freedom of religion.

Freedom of speech suits have sought to reduce the ability of correctional administrators to censor incoming and outgoing mail and to restrict communication among inmates. The general rule was enunciated in *Procunier v. Martinez* (1974). Censorship is permitted to the extent that it is necessary to maintain security of the facility, order in the institution, or treatment of inmates. The Supreme Court has held that a prisoner's mail may only be opened for legitimate reasons and that the procedure must be conducted in the least restrictive means possible. The Court addressed attorney-client privilege in *Wolfe v. McDonnell* (1974). While the Court indicated that the attorney client privilege must be respected, it did not absolutely restrict correctional officials from inspecting mail from attorneys. The Court permitted greater discretionary power to correctional officials regarding communications among inmates (*Vester v. Rogers*, 1986) when the communication may disrupt prison discipline. The *Procunier v. Martinez* (1974) and *Wolf v. McDonnell* (1974) decisions granted inmates considerable freedom from censorship by institutional authorities but left correctional authorities with the power to censor to the extent to which they could justify the restriction of the right in terms of institutional safety. Freedom of religion suits have sought permission for inmates to engage in a wide variety of behaviors identified with their religious beliefs which violated institutional regulations or practices. Requests have addressed dietary restrictions, grooming standards, working conditions, and drug use. In 1972, the United States Supreme Court opined in *Cruz v. Beto* that religious freedom must be granted to all religious faiths, in this case, Buddhism. While *Cruz* provided for religious recognition for all faiths, subsequent federal decisions have rejected the *Cruz* rationale in the cases of non-recognized faiths or faiths whose practice put an undue burden on institutional officials. Litigation in the area of religious freedom has continued and was amplified by the recently successfully challenged federal Religious Freedom Restoration Act. This issue will be thoroughly explored in Chapter 4.

Fourth Amendment Challenges. The Fourth Amendment protects people from unreasonable searches, seizures, and arrests. Most Fourth Amendment challenges assert that the inmates' right to privacy is being violated by unwarranted searches of their persons and property by prison officials.

In the Fourth Amendment arena, the Supreme Court has rendered several decisions which say, in effect, that inmates have a significantly lesser expectation of privacy than ordinary citizens. In *Hudson v. Palmer* (1984), the Supreme Court upheld a lower court ruling that allowed for the search of cells and the confiscation of any contraband found. The courts however have recognized some privacy for inmates. In 1981, the United States Court of Appeals for the Fourth Circuit ruled that inmates may not be strip searched by a guard or other official of the opposite sex, nor can officers of an opposite sex supervise bathing areas (*Lee v. Downs*, 1981).

While the courts have consistently held that inmates loose their right to protection from unwarranted searches by correctional officials (*U.S. v. Dawson*, 1975; *Hudson v. Palmer*, 1984; *U.S. v. Mills*, 1983), the courts have held that they are protected from wanton destruction of their personal effects (*Clifton v. Robinson*, 1980). While correctional officials retain the right to search visitors (*Smothers v. Gibson*, 1985; *Blackburn v. Snow*, 1985) and employees (*Security and Law Enforcement Employees District Council #82 v. Carey*, 1984; *U.S. v. York*, 1978), the extent of the search (strip and cavity searches) must be reasonable given the level of evidence available to support the belief that contraband is present.

Eighth Amendment Challenges. The Eighth Amendment prohibits excessive bail and fines and prohibits cruel and unusual punishments. Much of the early litigation that led to the breaking of the hands-off doctrine and much of the continuing litigation rests on alleged violations of the cruel and unusual punishment clause of the Eighth Amendment. Cases that have extended or clarified the extension of the Eighth Amendment in correctional environments have included the number of bunks in a cell (*Burks v. Walsh*, 1978; *Rhodes v. Chapman*, 1981) and the presence of tobacco smoke in the inmates' immediate environment (*Helling v. McKinney*, 1993). Cruel and unusual conditions identified in the key cases have also included inadequate heating coupled with inadequate clothing (to protect from cold), inadequate toilets, absence of mattresses, the presence of vermin such as rats and roaches, inadequate lighting, inadequate ventilation, intrusive surveillance, closed front cells, and crowding (Samaha, 1988). Eighth Amendment challenges to disciplinary standards and procedures will be addressed in Chapter 9.

Challenges to the death penalty as a breach of the cruel and unusual punishment provisions of the Eighth Amendment followed the initial breach of the hands-off doctrine with mixed results. In *Furman v. Georgia* (1972), the Supreme Court decided a case that challenged the death penalty as a violation of the cruel and unusual punishment provisions of the Eighth Amendment. The decision held the application of the death penalty to be unconstitutional on the basis of unbridled discretion granted to state court juries in assigning the death penalty. Georgia revised its statute to remove discretion from the sentencing process in capital cases. In *Gregg v. Georgia* (1976), executions authorized under the new statute were held to be in compliance with the Eighth Amendment. Death row conditions challenges continue to be brought forward and are covered in Chapter 6. The court has vacillated on a collateral issue, admissibility of victim statements at the sentencing hearing. These statements were excluded in *Booth v. Maryland* (1987) and *Gathers v. South Carolina* (1989) but held to be a matter of states' rights in *Payne v. Tennessee* (1991).

Fourteenth Amendment Challenges. The Fourteenth Amendment guarantees equal protection under the law and due process in legal proceedings. Much of the litigation advanced under Fourteenth Amendment challenges reference specific federal statutes that prohibit discrimination. Cases include gender discrimination in the provision of resources (*Glover v. Johnson,* 1979) and access to legal materials and assistance (*Bounds v. Smith,* 1977). Inmate legal access will be addressed more completely in the pages to follow as will discrimination.

Statutory Challenges

Three federal statutes tend to dominate actions filed in federal court: Section 2674 of the Federal Torts Claims Act of 1946, Section 1983 of the Civil Rights Act, and the Federal Habeas Corpus Act. These statutes frequently provide the vehicle by which allegations of violations of constitutional rights are brought to the federal court.

Section 2674. Complaints under Section 2674 of the Federal Tort Claims Act of 1946 were made available to inmates in federal correctional institutions in 1963 (*United States v. Muniz,* 1963). Under the Federal Tort Claims Act, plaintiffs seek compensation for damages resulting from inappropriate actions of federal agencies and employees.

Section 1983 of Title 42. Section 1983 of the Civil Rights Act allows recovery of damages or injunctive relief when a constitutional right is violated by a public official acting in his or her official capacity (Hawkins & Alpert, 1989). Injunctive relief is more likely to be granted than monetary damages awarded (Rudovsky, Bronstein, Koren & Cade, 1983). The statute also allows inmates to challenge the conditions of incarceration by alleging that the cited conditions violate the inmates' civil rights. The statute also permits class action suits (Gobert & Cohen, 1981). Suits alleging violations of First, Fifth, and Fourteenth Amendments have been effectively advanced under Section 1983 complaints (Krantz, 1983). An expansion of the Civil Rights Act, the Civil Rights of Institutionalized Persons Act, can be used by prisoners although it was designed primarily for the protection of mental health patients (Henak, 1982). This act recognizes that institutionalized people are particularly vulnerable to abuse of constitutional rights. Actions under this act must be brought by the U.S. Attorney General.

Federal Habeas Corpus Act. Congress extended federal habeas corpus relief to state inmates in 1867. The Federal Habeas Corpus Act grants relief if the plaintiff can establish that the statute under which he or she was convicted was unconstitutional, his or her constitutional rights were violated during the trial process, or that he or she is being held in the wrong institution (Krantz, 1983). Inmates who seek to challenge their conviction or sentence seek relief under the Federal Habeas Corpus Act. The Act is the vehicle through which some constitutional challenges are brought before the court. In *Coffin v. Reichard* (1944) the court ruled that Federal Habeas Corpus Act could be applied to the conditions of confinement as well as to the accuracy of the conviction and subsequent incarceration.

Contemporary Access to the Court

Recently, the Supreme Court reaffirmed its policy regarding the limits that can be placed on an inmate's access to the judicial process. In *O'Sullivan v. Boerckel* (1999), an Illinois inmate sought federal relief for his state convictions for aggravated battery, burglary, and rape. The intermediate state appellate court affirmed his convictions. Boerckel then petitioned the Illinois Supreme Court to review his case and raised three grounds as his basis for relief: unlawful arrest and confession, prosecutorial misconduct, and a discovery violation. The state supreme court denied the petition.

Boerckel then sought federal habeas relief. In this petition, Boerckel raised six issues. In addition to the issues he raised at the state level, he raised ineffective assistance of counsel, a Miranda violation, and a claim that the evidence was insufficient to support his conviction. The U.S. District Court found procedural default by Boerckel on the issues he failed to raise in his discretionary petition to the Illinois Supreme Court. The Seventh Circuit Court of Appeals, however, reversed the district court, finding that Boerckel need not have presented those issues at the state level in a petition for discretionary review in order to meet the federal exhaustion requirement.

Justice O'Connor, however, writing for the six member majority, held that the inmate must first absolutely exhaust his state remedies before turning to the federal courts for assistance. State courts must be given a fair opportunity to resolve a petitioner's claim of federal constitutional rights violations before federal relief is pursued.

Summary

Historically, states' rights have taken precedence over inmate rights in challenges to the management of state institutions. The hands-off doctrine was well established in the 1800s and remained an established doctrine until the 1960s. Organized inmate rights groups brought pressure to bear on departments of corrections across the United States. This pressure, coupled with severe conditions in the prisons of Arkansas and Alabama, provided a context in which the hands-off doctrine could not stand.

The original decisions, which were extensive and specific in terms of conditions and standards, were district court decisions that survived in principle on appeal by state and correctional officials named as defendants. Once the hands-off doctrine was breached on the basis of the Cruel and Unusual Punishment Clause of the Eighth Amendment, federal interest in a broad array of inmate rights had been established. Violations of the First, Fourth, Eighth, and Fourteenth Amendments have been brought forward independently and through the use of various federal statutes such as the Federal Habeas Corpus Act, the Civil Rights Act, and the Federal Torts Claims Act.

The new standard that has been advanced focuses on the attitudes of the correctional administrators and asserts that these managers must demonstrate deliberate indifference toward the inmate or his or her circumstances. The breach of the hands-off doctrine has produced the filing of a great number of complaints in the federal courts by inmates, many of which appear to be frivolous on their face. The system is attempting to adapt. The issue of the limitations on inmate rights is still to be decided. The cases accepted for review by the United States Supreme Court and the decisions rendered in the coming years will continue to influence the administration of correctional institutions in the various states of this country. Until the fundamental issue—to what extent can the state restrict the rights of those it chooses to isolate from society—is adequately addressed, court-ordered standards for the administration of correctional institutions will continue to evolve and prevail.

The following chapters of this book will address a number of areas in which litigation continues to be relatively active. Issues addressed will include access to the courts, legal materials, and legal assistance; the impact of the Prison Litigation Reform Act; religious freedom and the impact of the recently successfully challenged Religious Freedom Restoration Act; sentencing reform acts and the death penalty and death row conditions; privatization of prisons and prison services; standards of medical care; restrictions on inmate discipline and inmate control; and special restrictions on sexual offenders. We will conclude with a look to the future.

References

Butler, D. (1993). Cruel and unusual punishment takes one step forward, two steps back. Denver University Law Review , 70, 393-412.

Gobert, J.L., & Cohen, N.P. (1981). *Rights of Prisoners*. Colorado Sprigs, CO: McGraw- Hill.

Hawkins, R., & Alpert, G.P. (1989). *American Prison Systems: Punishment and justice*. Englewood Cliffs, NJ: Prentice Hall.

Henak, R.P. (1982). *Prisoners' rights. An annual survey of American law*. Dobbs Ferry, NY: Ocean Publications.

Krantz, S. (1983). *Corrections and prisoners' rights*. St. Paul, MN: West Publishing.

Mohs, D. (1993). Opening and closing the door to Eighth Amendment excessive force claims. *Saint Louis University Law Journal , 37*, 489-498.

Montick, D. (1983). Challenging cruel and unusual conditions of prison confinement: Refining the totality of conditions approach. *Howard Law Review , 26*, 227-266.

Murton, T., & Hyams, J. (1969). *Accomplices to the crime*. New York: Grove Press.

Palmer, J. (1991). *Constitutional rights of prisoners*. Cincinnati: Anderson.

Rudovsky, D., Bronstein, A.J., Koran, E.I., & Cade, J. (1988). *The rights of Prisoners: The basic ACLU guide to prisoner's rights*. Carbondale, IL: Southern Illionis University Press.

Samaha, J. (1988). *Criminal justice*. Saint Paul, MN: West.

Smollo, R. (1984). Prison overcrowding and the courts: A road map for the 1980's. *University of Illinois Law Review*, 1984, 399-421.

Cases

Blackburn v. Snow, 771 F. 2d 556 (1985)

Booth v. Maryland, 482 U.S. 496 (1987)

Bounds v. Smith, 430 U.S. 817 (1977)

Burks v. Walsh, 461 F. Supp. 454 (W.D. MO 1978)

Clifton v. Robinson, 500 F. Supp. 30 (1980)

Coffin v. Reichard, 143 F. 2d 443 (1944)

Cooper v. Pate, 378 U.S. 546 (1964)

Cruz v. Beto, 405 U.S. 319 (1972)

Estelle v. Gamble, 429 U.S. 27 (1976)

Ex parte Hull, 312 U.S. 546 (1941)

Farmer v. Brennan, 511 U.S. 825 (1994)

Furman v. Georgia, 408 U.S. 238 (1972)

Gathers v. South Carolina, 490 U.S. 805 (1989)

Glover v. Johnson, 478 F. Supp. 1075 (1979)

Gore v. United States, 357 U.S. 386 (1958)

Gregg v. Georgia, 428 U.S. 153 (1976)

Helling v. McKinney, 509 U.S. 25 (1993)

Holt v. Sarver, 300 F. Supp. 825 (M.D. Ark. 1969)

Hudson v. McMillian, 112 S. Ct. 995 (1992)

Hudson v. Palmer, 468 U.S. 517 (1984)

Jackson v. Bishop, 404 F. 2d 571 (1968)

Lee v. Downs, 641 F. 2d 1117 (1981)

Martinez v. Rosado, 474 F. Supp. 758 (S.D. NY 1979)

Newman v. Alabama, 349 F. Supp. 278 (M.D. Ala. 1972)

O'Sullivan v. Boerckel, 119 S. Ct. 1728 (1999)

Payne v. Tennessee, 501 U.S. 808 (1991)

Pervear v. Massachusetts, 72 U.S. 678 (1866)

Procunier v. Martinez, 416 U.S. 396 (1974)

Pugh v. Locke, 406 F. Supp. 318 (M.D. AL 1976)

Rhodes v. Chapman, 452 U.S. 337 (1981)

Ruffin v. Commonwealth, 62 Va. 790 (1871)

Security and Law Enforcement Employees District Council #82
     v. Carey, 737 F. 2d 187(1984)

Smothers v. Gibson, 778 F. 2d 470 (1985)

Talley v. Stevens, 247 F. Supp. 683 (M.D. Aka. 1965)

U.S. v. Dawson, 516 F. 2d 796 (9th Cir. 1975)

U.S. v. Mills, 704 F. 2d 1553 (1983)

U.S. v. Muniz, 374 U.S. 150 (1963)

U.S. v. York, 578 F. 2d 1036 (1978)

Vester v. Rogers, 795 F. 2d 1179 (1986)

Wilson v. Seiter, 501 U.S. 294 (1991)

Wolfe v. McDonnell, 418 U.S. 539 (1974)

Chapter 2

Lewis and Casey and Inmate Access to the Courts

In the last decade, citizen outrage over increasing crime rates has resulted in a move to increase the use and length of prison sentences and to reduce the rights and privileges enjoyed by incarcerated persons. One area often cited by critics of the system involves inmate litigation challenging various aspects of confinement. The plethora of lawsuits filed by inmates in this area has brought the issue of inmate access to the courts back into the spotlight. Of these issues, access to the courts and adequate representation have been the most challenged. Recent decisions have continued to refine the standards for housing inmates that must be met to assure minimum compliance with constitutional standards.

Access to the courts has persistently been held to be a fundamental right extended to all who find themselves within the borders of the United States regardless of their status. Inmates are one class of people who live in environments that are legitimately designed to restrict the free expression of many of their rights as a part of the penalty which they are expected to pay for violation of the rules that society has established to assure a relatively stable, fair, and safe environment for all members of the society. This restrictive nature of the prison environment has a chilling effect on any effort to assert rights. Asserting rights challenges authority, authority that is perceived by most correctional professionals to be essential to the safe management of the correctional institution. While the intentional denial of access to the courts is relatively rare today, practices are designed to protect the institution from disruption and to maintain a safe controlled environment. Censorship, the control of contraband, and firm aggressive imposition of inmate management procedures block free access to legal materials and legal assistance usually without a specific intent to interfere with legitimate access to the courts as will be discussed in Chapter 9. The lack of financial resources and the limited educational achievements of most prison inmates further reduce effective access to the courts. Taxpayers are reluctant to provide funds for many of the amenities enjoyed by most citizens and are certainly reluctant to provide expensive legal assistance to prisoners. As a result, unqualified assistance (jailhouse lawyers) has been accepted even though most correctional administrators believe that providing any group of inmates with an effective power base leads to abuse of other inmates and a reduction in the ability of the staff to control the institution. Correctional managers also see most suits as unfounded and a tool in the hands of manipulative inmates who seek to reduce the extent to which the correctional managers control the institutional environment. They are hesitant to do anything that would increase the ability of inmates to control the institution, and they resist the expenditure of state funds to support efforts that they perceive to be frivolous and disruptive. As a result, correctional managers seek standards and procedures that minimally comply with constitutional requirements. As the boundaries are not clear, litigation continues as the line between minimally acceptable standards and resources and unacceptable standards and resources is tested.

The first major U.S. Supreme Court decision regarding prisoner access to the courts was *Ex parte Hull* (1941). In *Hull*, the detainee, Cleio Hull, was convicted of a sexual offense and sentenced to an indeterminate sentence. After 10 months, he was paroled, only to be convicted again approximately one year later for a similar offense. This conviction drew a sentence of 36 to 60 months. In 1940, Hull prepared a habeas petition along with exhibits for the U.S. Supreme Court. Hull took the papers to be notarized by a prison official; however, prison officials refused to notarize his papers, and he was informed that his papers as prepared were unacceptable. Hull then attempted to send the papers out of the institution by his father; however, the papers were confiscated by correctional officials. Soon thereafter, Hull attempted to send another letter to the clerk of the U.S. Supreme Court. This time the legal request for a hearing was not mailed, but was sent to the parole board with a request for the parole board to determine whether Hull should receive a new trial (*Ex parte Hull*, 1941). In essence, the parole board was asked to rule on the merits of Hull's complaint.

Hull challenged, on constitutional grounds, the Michigan Department of Corrections policy that required that all inmate federal habeas petitions be submitted to correctional authorities for review by an "investigator" for parole board approval before being filed with the court. The U.S. Supreme Court held that such requirements were invalid because it adversely affected a prisoner's ability to seek redress to which he or she was entitled.

Subsequent to *Hull*, the Court in *Johnson v. Avery* (1969) invalidated a Tennessee prohibition against jailhouse lawyers, and observed that nearly all prisoners are effectively denied access to the courts unless some assistance, such as the jailhouse lawyer, is available. Johnson was serving a sentence of life without the possibility of parole. Department of Corrections policy specifically stated that no inmate could receive assistance from any other inmate in preparation of legal claims. In 1965, Johnson filed a "Motion For Law Books and A Typewriter" so that he could prepare an effective complaint challenging his assignment to disciplinary segregation in the maximum-security cellblock. The trial court held that the prohibition on assistance was unconstitutional in that it in effect barred illiterate prisoners from filing effective federal habeas petitions. The court recognized that the correctional managers' argument that permitting jailhouse lawyers to provide assistance placed these inmates in a position of power that they could use to exploit other prisoners and disrupt the institutional environment was valid, but held that the right of access to such legal assistance as was available in the correctional environment was more important (*Johnson v. Avery*, 1969).

Jailhouse lawyers, as Milovanovic and Thomas (1989) have observed, make a career out of law. These individuals attempt to seize upon one inmate's situation and transform it into a legal issue that will result in a sweeping effect throughout an entire institution or department of corrections. Of course, these individuals are in no way licensed to practice law in the traditional sense; however, given the lack of resources available in a vast majority of institutions to provide legal assistance for inmates, their roles are becoming more and more important and their impact substantial. As a result, correctional authorities, who saw the substantial increase in litigation as frivolous, generated policies designed to limit the scope of jailhouse lawyers to replace polices absolutely prohibiting access to jailhouse lawyers in an attempt to maintain firm control of the correctional environment. Early litigation (*Novak v. Beto*, 1971) produced a finding that systems designed to replace jailhouse lawyers must be effective. In this case, the provision of two paid attorneys was held to be insufficient to meet the needs of inmates for legal assistance. A second decision, *Williams v. The Department of Justice*, (1970) held that the use of law students as a substitute for access to jailhouse lawyers was not adequate when a period of 18 months elapsed between the request for assistance and the first interview. The *Hull* line of cases culminated in 1977 with the U.S. Supreme Court's mandate in the case of *Bounds v. Smith* (1977) which stated that departments of corrections must provide inmates with meaningful avenues of access to the courts.

From *Johnson* to *Bounds*:
The Scope of Inmate Access Considered

In *Younger v. Gilmore* (1971), the U.S. Supreme Court sustained, *per curiam*, the findings of the Ninth Circuit Court of

Appeals, *Lynch v. Gilmore* (1968). Consistent with the United States Constitution, states must protect the right of prisoners to access the courts by providing them with law libraries or alternative sources of legal assistance sufficient to permit effective access to the courts; but, as Hinckley (1987) has noted, the lead cases only concerned inmate access to the courts in the context of federal habeas corpus petitions and the interference by institutional officials with a limited interpretation of that constitutional right. Consequently, some state departments of corrections continued to place burdensome restrictions on inmates' ability to seek redress in areas outside the federal habeas context.

When this practice was challenged, the U.S. Supreme Court, in *Wolfe v. McDonnell* (1974), held that the right of inmate access to the courts extended beyond the mere ability to file federal habeas claims. Incarcerated individuals had a constitutional right to file claims apart from habeas corpus petitions and to receive assistance from jailhouse counsel in preparation of those claims in areas such as Section 1983 civil rights actions. The Court observed that the line of separation between civil rights actions and habeas petitions is not always clear (*Wolfe v. McDonnell*, 1974). Thus, the important focus of the constitutionally protected right of access to the courts is not on the ultimate result of the habeas action which seeks release as opposed to the civil rights claim which more commonly seeks relief from undesirable environmental conditions in correctional institutions. The point is that both the habeas corpus action and the civil rights action serve to protect an inmate's constitutional or federally legislated rights.

Now that inmates had the right to file almost any claim they chose regarding their confinement, the question remained as to what extent inmates were entitled to assistance in preparation of those claims. The Court wasted little time directly addressing this issue.

Bounds v. Smith and
the Institutional Law Library

The answer as to what extent inmates were guaranteed access to the courts came, at least in part, in *Bounds v. Smith* (1977). Under consideration in *Bounds* was a North Carolina Department of Corrections (NCDOC) proposal designed to settle the complaint before the Court for providing seven institutional law libraries, located within prisons throughout the state, as well as smaller research facilities in specialized units, including the segregation unit and the women's facility. Prior to litigation in the courts below, there was only one prison law library available to the entire inmate population of the seventy-seven correctional units in the state.

Under the NCDOC proposal, with the additional libraries, inmates could request a scheduled appointment to use the legal research facilities. This plan provided seven institutional libraries instead of one for the seventy-seven institutions. Under the proposal, inmates in correctional institutions without libraries were to be transported to and housed in institutions with libraries and allowed adequate time in the library to prepare their legal claims. In each facility, there were to be legal texts, form books, paper, pens, typewriters, and copying machines. NCDOC-trained inmates would serve as research assistants and typists to assist fellow inmates.

Despite the state's efforts to improve inmate access to the courts by way of independent legal research and drafting, inmates challenged these provisions as being grossly insufficient and sought establishment of a library at every prison; however, the district court found that the library plan was sufficient to give the inmates reasonable access to the courts. The U.S. Supreme Court agreed with this decision, stating, "while adequate law libraries are *one* [emphasis added] constitutionally acceptable way to assure meaningful access to the courts, our decision here [in *Bounds*]...does not foreclose alternative means to achieve the goal" (*Bounds* at 830) In short, experimentation in various methods of providing inmate access to the courts by state departments of corrections was encouraged by the Court. *Bounds* can be read to suggest that there is no one universal solution. That is, different conditions in different states might require different solutions to provide effective access. One case has held that the provision of law libraries in and of itself is not adequate. In *Hooks v. Wainwright* (1982), the Court held providing libraries to be staffed with law clerks and librarians was not sufficient without access to licensed attorneys to provide effective access to the courts. It can be noted that, in this case, a substantial proportion of the inmate population was Hispanic lacking basic skills needed to read and understand law texts written in English and that a substantial proportion of the correctional population was functionally illiterate.

Clearly, law libraries were one acceptable method of meeting the *Bounds* access requirements in most cases; however, it became equally clear that, as Smith (1987) has noted, the substantial reliance upon prison law libraries as the sole means to provide effective access to the courts was doomed to failure. Simply providing a law library for inmates does not substitute for the ability to read and write and conduct legal research, skills vital to effectively pursuing legal claims. The most recent litigation has made clear that law libraries are not the only method for protecting the inmate's right to access to the courts. Moreover, law libraries may not now be the best of many other alternatives.

Lewis v. Casey: A Brief Overview

The U.S. Supreme Court revisited the right of inmate access to the courts in *Lewis v. Casey* (1996). *Casey* went to the Court on appeal by the State of Arizona, which challenged the rulings of the U.S. Court of Appeals for the Ninth Circuit and the U.S. District Court for Arizona.

The U.S. District Court for Arizona issued a broad, sweeping condemnation of the Arizona prison system. Specifically, this case encompassed a class challenge alleging that inmates were being denied access to the courts. In its remedy, the district court, in painstaking and meticulous detail, set forth how the institutional libraries were to be run. The order covered everything from hours of operation to providing telephone access for inmate conferral with counsel. The Ninth Circuit affirmed, and the State of Arizona sought relief.

In a nutshell, the U.S. Supreme Court made the following observations regarding inmate access in *Casey*:

1) A successful systemic challenge turns on the demonstration of widespread and actual injury;

2) *Bounds* did not create an abstract, freestanding right to institutional law libraries. (The right that *Bounds* acknowledged was the right of access to the courts.);

3) To establish a *Bounds* violation, the inmate must demonstrate actual injury in that the quality of the legal research facilities or other legal assistance programs is hindering efforts to file a non-frivolous legal claim;

4) Institutional authorities are under no constitutional obligation to assist inmates in discovering grievances and presenting them to a court; and,

5) *Bounds* in no way guaranteed the ability of inmates to file any and every claim, but requires only that the inmates be given the ability to directly and collaterally attack their sentences and to challenge conditions of confinement.

Inmate Access after *Lewis v. Casey*: *Bounds* Significantly Modified and the States' Constitutional Duty to Provide Inmate Access Clarified

The U.S. Supreme Court's decision in *Lewis v. Casey* is best considered in its individual parts.[1] In short, the *Casey* majority held that an individual inmate's ability to attack a prison system's access program for inmates turns on his or her standing to challenge the program and that lower courts must defer to prison authorities on matters of institutional administration.

Challenges to Inmate Access Programs Ultimately Turns On Standing

The State of Arizona's fundamental contention was that the U.S. District Court's findings were inadequate on two fronts to justify a system-wide remedy (*Lewis v. Casey*, 1996). First, the State argued that for a *Bounds* access violation, inmates had to show that the alleged deficiencies in the legal program had resulted in actual injury. Second, the State contended that there were insufficient findings of actual injury to warrant such a sweeping remedy.

The Court rested this portion of its opinion on the constitutional doctrine of standing, which prevents courts from undertaking tasks assigned to other parts of the government. The Court, per Justice Scalia, noted that absent this constitutional

---

1. The Court divided its opinion into three parts. Scalia, J. issued the three part opinion, in which Rehnquist, C.J., and O'Connor, Kennedy, and Thomas, JJ. joined as to all parts. Souter, Ginsburg, and Breyer, JJ. joined parts I and III and concurred in judgment. Thomas, J. issued a separate concurring opinion, and Stevens, J. dissented as to all parts. Thus, Part I of the opinion was 8-1, Part II was 5-4, and Part III was 8-1.

principle, the lines of responsibility between the various branches of government would be destroyed:

> In the context of the present case: [i]t is for the courts to remedy past or imminent official interference with individual inmates' presentation of claims to the courts; it is for the political branches of the State and Federal governments to manage prisons in such a fashion that official interference with the presentation of claims will not occur. Of course, the two roles briefly and partially coincide when a court... [grants relief to an inmate or class of inmates]. But the distinction between the two roles would be obliterated if, to invoke intervention of the courts, no actual or imminent harm were needed, but merely the status of being subject to a governmental institution that was not organized or managed properly. (*Lewis v. Casey*, 1996 at 2179)

Based on this approach to the issue, the Court maintained its cautious approach in refusing to micromanage state institutions. The Court further noted that the standing issue was forced by the inmates' claims based on their erroneous assumption that they had a constitutional right to law libraries and legal assistance in preparing claims, "[b]ut *Bounds* established no such right.... The right that *Bounds* acknowledged was the (already well-established) right of access to the courts."

The standing issue was further addressed in *Stumes v. Bloomberg* (1996), where the South Dakota Supreme Court rejected an inmate's claim challenging the appropriations to the state prison system. The inmate asserted standing on the basis of the fact that he was a taxpayer. The court, however, dismissed this notion, asserting that once the inmate entered the prison gates, he ceased to be a taxpayer.

The Supreme Court continued, emphasizing that *Bounds* only said that law libraries were one method of providing inmate access. Thus,

> [b]ecause *Bounds* did not create an abstract, freestanding right to a law library or legal assistance, an inmate cannot

establish relevant actual injury simply by establishing that his prison's law library or legal assistance program is sub-par in some theoretical sense. (*Lewis v. Casey,* 1996 at 2180)

While *Bounds* made no mention of actual injury, that showing is now required. The Court noted that the actual injury requirement was implied in the *Bounds* decision by that Court's encouragement of state experimentation in this area. Importantly, the *Casey* Court suggests that law libraries may be eliminated completely and replaced with "some minimal access to legal advice and a system of court-provided forms...." Further, the Court noted that such experimentation was not encouraged simply for suggestion's sake. *Casey* establishes that a new experimental program should remain in place until an inmate is successful in demonstrating that a *non-frivolous* legal claim had been prevented because of the program. At least one court has held that a parole board's consideration of an inmate's litigation activity cannot, per se, be bootstrapped to a claim of retaliation when parole is denied (*Johnson v. Rodriguez,* 1997). The plaintiff-inmate claimed that the consideration of his litigation effectively denied him access to the courts because if he pursued his claims, he would be denied parole. But, the court rejected this notion, holding that the consideration of frivolous filings by the inmate or filings unrelated to the complaining inmate's case could not form the basis for a retaliation charge. To be successful in his claim, the inmate would have to had demonstrated that he engaged in constitutionally protected litigation activity, was denied parole, and that the denial of parole was in an effort to limit his ability to pursue his claims.

The actual injury requirement of *Casey* has been the clear focal point of appellate courts in inmate access decisions rendered subsequent to *Casey.* Even though an inmate-plaintiff may demonstrate a total lack of an access mechanism in a particular institution, unless he can show that the lack of access resulted in dismissal or other prejudice to his legal claim, then he has no claim of lack of access to the courts (*Bass v. Singletary,* 1998; *Klinger v. Department of Corrections,* 1997; *Sabers v. Delano,*

1996; *Pilgrim v. Littlefield,* 1996). Further, challenge to a prison policy prohibiting physical contact with the inmate's wife/paralegal was found not to be unduly burdensome to the inmate's ability to contact his legal team or otherwise seek legal redress (*O'Dell v. Netherland,* 1997). Again, the inmate in this case was unable to demonstrate that the prison regulation caused him actual prejudice in pursuing a legal claim. Furthermore, this court suggested that even had the inmate demonstrated an interference with access to the courts by this policy, there were sufficient other alternatives available for him to pursue his claims. Additionally, the claim of denial of access to the courts must not be vague. In order to be successful, the inmate lodging the allegation must specifically plead and prove how he was harmed by the alleged denial of access (*Parkhurst v. Uphoff,* 1997).

The Supreme Court's standing analysis in *Casey* continued, noting that *Bounds* went beyond the right of access recognized in previous decisions, in that it allowed that prisoners have a right to present any grievance that they wish to file. This seems to suggest that institutions are required to assist inmates in discovering claims and in assuring that the inmates are effective litigators and to that end, that portion of the compliant is disclaimed in *Casey.* The Court pointed out that to confer such a broad right upon inmates was largely academic since the vast majority of inmates are uneducated and illiterate. While broad sweeping decrees granting programs and services to inmates by the lower federal courts may contain desirable benefits, judicial dictates of this nature are inappropriate (*Women Prisoners of the District of Columbia v. District of Columbia,* 1996).

Finally, on the point of standing, the Court limited the venues in which the actual injury requirement could be satisfied, noting that frustration of any legal claim would not suffice:

> ...*Bounds* does not guarantee inmates the wherewithal to transform themselves into litigating engines.... *The tools it requires be provided are those that the inmates need in order to attack their sentences, directly or collaterally, and in order to challenge the conditions of their confinement. Impairment of*

other litigating capacity is simply one of the incidental (and perfectly constitutional) consequences of conviction and incarceration [emphasis added]. (*Lewis v. Casey,* 1996 at 2182)

While this *Casey* dictate may seem harsh, in reality it is not. Writ-writers have no independent right to provide other inmates legal advice, but they may assert that right for others who otherwise would not have an opportunity to have their claims addressed (*Tighe v. Wall,* 1996). But, absent the demonstration of an actual prejudice to a legal filing, no denial of access can survive. Officials may even ban legal correspondence between inmates in different units for security purposes without trampling an inmate's right of access to the courts; however, the failure to return an inmate's legal materials from a writ-writer who is transferred to another unit does violate the inmate's right of access to the courts (*Tucker v. Graves,* 1997; *Goff v. Nix,* 1997). Inmates, pursuant to *Casey,* do have the right to enforce a judgment once it is obtained (*Plyler v. Moore,* 1996).

The Court concluded its standing analysis by stating that the district court's finding of actual injury was insufficient to warrant such a broad remedy, noting "... the Constitution does not require that prisoners (literate or illiterate) be able to conduct generalized research." Several post-*Casey* decisions have made this point. In *Tokar v. Armontrout* (1996) and *Yahweh v. Zavaras* (1996), the courts held that there is no constitutional right to physical access to a law library simply to flip pages and seek out claims. Another court, however, reversed a lower court's summary judgment in favor of the institution where an inmate challenged the idle pay system of the institution (*Meyers v. Hundley,* 1996). Under the system, inmates were allowed $7.70 per month for personal hygiene items, non-prescription medications, and stamps and supplies for legal mailings. The plaintiff-inmate in this case offered proof that a lack of funds caused him to miss a filing deadline.

Additionally, many inmate claims attacking an institution's access to courts programs allege that deprivation of photocopies of materials prejudices their ability to pursue their legal grievances; however, pursuant to *Casey,* courts have held that unless an inmate can demonstrate that the denial of the photocopied materials has caused prejudice to the filing of a legal claim, then no relief is warranted *(Hiser v. Franklin*, 1996; *Graham v. Baxter,* 1996; *Nance v. Vieregge*, 1998). At least one state court, however, has declined to impose the actual injury requirement of *Casey*, holding that challenges to institutional policies only need show that the policy was motivated by an intent to limit court access (*Mathis v. Sauser*, 1997).

Courts Must Defer to the Judgment of Prison Authorities on Matters of Institutional Administration

The Court was nearly unanimous in its finding that institutional administration is the business of prison administrators and not judges. In *Turner v. Safley* (1987), the Court held that an institutional regulation impinging on inmates' constitutional rights is appropriate if it is reasonably related to proper correctional interests. In *Turner*, the class action suit challenged the intra-institutional correspondence regulations between inmates and the prison's marital policy. Justice O'Connor, writing for the Court, noted that prison operations are a function of the legislative and executive branches of government, and when an institutional regulation touches a constitutional right, the regulation will not be invalidated unless it is not rationally related to a legitimate prison concern. Whether alternative means of exercising a particular right aside from the challenged regulation, the impact that an accommodation for the complaining inmate would place on institutional workers, and whether or not there are acceptable alternative means for exercising the right are all relevant factors in considering the reasonableness of a regulation (*Turner v. Safley,* 1987).

The *Casey* Court held that *Bounds* must now be read in conjunction with *Turner* in that both of those cases have a common purpose—namely reasonableness in institutional regulations. As a result of *Turner*, it has been held that one envelope per week is sufficient to give an inmate access to the courts (*Hershberger v. Scaletta*, 1994). More recently, the Arkansas Supreme Court reached this same conclusion (*Rowbottom v. State*, 1997). Additionally, an inmate alleging deprivation of supplies as a cause of his being denied access to the courts must show that the lack of supplies caused him actual prejudice in filing a claim (*Guinn v. Zavaras*, 1996).

In another case, the inmate-plaintiff challenged his inability to increase the number of persons on his approved phone list. The institutional policy allowed for inmates to have 10 names on a phone list that could be changed every 6 months. The district court ordered the number be increased to 15, but the circuit court of appeals reversed, noting that the prison's policy was reasonable and that federal courts must recognize their roles in prison regulation and not overstep their boundaries (*Pope v. Hightower*, 1996). Similarly, the Connecticut Supreme Court found that the state prison's telephone policy did not unduly burden the inmate's ability to contact his attorneys; however, this case was resolved on state constitutional grounds with strong rhetoric analogizing this case to the holding in *Casey* (*Washington v. Meachum*, 1996).

The district court's remedy in *Casey* was "inordinately—indeed, wildly—intrusive. *Bounds* represented the epitome of what should be done in matters such as this, while the District Court's remedy here was the model of what should not be done."

Summary

The controversy over the nature of inmate access to the courts represents conflict among differing legitimate and illegitimate interests in the correctional setting. The main parties are correctional administrators who have a legitimate interest in maintaining a controlled and stable institutional environment, inmates who have a legitimate interest in seeking remedies to improper conviction or a legitimate interest in resisting the denial of a right, and inmates who have an illegitimate interest in reducing the ability of correctional administrators to effectively control and maintain a safe stable institutional environment. Correctional administrators have a legitimate interest in restricting access to the courts when inmates bring frivolous complaints forward which appear to have little value other than the frustration of legitimate efforts of correctional administrators to manage the institution. They can also be expected to seek the least expensive method of providing the resources that they are obligated to provide. In the process of reducing the ability of inmates to file frivolous complaints, correctional managers cannot interfere with the ability of inmates to file legitimate complaints. The difference between a frivolous and a legitimate complaint is, at times, a matter of contention. The impact of recent decisions has been to set the bar a bit higher for inmates with legitimate complaints and to reduce the number of frivolous complaints that will survive the process.

While there is clearly a right of access to the courts guaranteed to inmates, the U.S. Supreme Court, federal courts of appeal, and state appellate courts are clearly moving toward further restricting the prisoner's ability to bring suits on a whim. It is, however, equally apparent that while these courts are more closely scrutinizing inmate claims, the judiciary remains sensitive to the fact that inmates do need an avenue to seek relief for constitutional violations. While *Casey* is strong in rhetoric, the effect of the decision simply requires prisoner-plaintiffs to demonstrate an actual harm in pursuing non-frivolous legal claims. While further restrictions may come in the future, for now, the inmate's ability to seek relief is alive and well.

Based on the Court's rationale in *Casey*, it is clear that law libraries are but one of an array of methods of providing inmate access. States are encouraged to experiment and if the Court strictly adheres to *Casey*, programs employed by state departments of corrections will not be summarily abolished without a showing of actual injury by a complaining inmate. More importantly, the Court is clearly locked into the notion that federal courts should not meddle in the internal workings of state correctional institutions and that substantial deference should be granted state departments of corrections where their programs serve important penological goals. It appears that state departments of corrections may now completely close institutional law libraries and substitute other legal assistance programs so long as meaningful and timely access is provided to inmates.

References

Hinckley, S. D. (1987). Bounds and beyond: A need to reevaluate the right of prisoner access to the courts. *University of Richmond Law Review, 22,* 19-49.

Milovanovic, D., & Thomas, J. (1989). Overcoming the absurd: Prisoner litigation as primitive rebellion. *International Journal of the Sociology of Law, 16,* 455-475.

Smith, C. E. (1987). Examining the boundaries of bounds: Prison law libraries and access to the courts. *Howard Law Journal, 30,* 27-44.

Cases

Bass v. Singletary, 143 F. 3d 1442 (11th Cir. 1998)

Bounds v. Smith, 430 U.S. 817 (1977)

Ex parte Hull, 312 U.S. 546 (1942)

Goff v. Nix, 113 F. 3d 887 (8th Cir. 1997)

Graham v. Baxter, No. 96-1241, 1996 WL 723340 (10th Cir. December 17, 1996)

Guinn v. Zavaras, No. 96-1179, 1996 WL 623239 (10th Cir. October 29, 1996)

Hershberger v. Scaletta, 33 F. 3d 955 (8th Cir. 1994)

Hiser v. Franklin, 94 F. 3d 1287 (9th Cir. 1996)

Hooks v. Wainwright, 536 F. Supp. 1330 (M.D. Fla. 1982) (overruled by 775 F. 2d 1443 (11th cir. 1985))

Johnson v. Avery, 393 U.S. 483 (1969)

Johnson v. Rodriguez, 110 F. 3d 299 (5th Cir. 1997)

Klinger v. Department of Corrections, 107 F. 3d 609 (8th Cir. 1997)

Lewis v. Casey, 116 S. Ct. 2174 (1996)

Lynch v. Gilmore, 400 F. 2d 228 (9th Cir. 1968)

Mathis v. Sauser, 942 P. 2d 1117 (Alak. 1997)

Meyers v. Hundley, 101 F. 3d 542 (8th Cir. 1996)

Nance v. Vieregge, 147 F. 3d 589 (7th Cir. 1998)

Novak v. Beto, 453 F. 2d 661 (5th Cir. 1971)

O'Dell v. Netterland, 112 F. 3d 773 (4th Cir. 1997)

Parkhurst v. Uphoff, No. 95-8003, 1997 WL 139766 (10th Cir. March 27, 1997)

Pilgrim v. Littlefield, 92 F. 3d 413 (6th Cir. 1996)

Plyler v. Moore, 100 F. 3d 365 (4th Cir. 1996)

Pope v. Hightower, 101 F. 3d 1382 (11th Cir. 1996)

Rowbottom v. State, 938 S.W. 2d 224 (Ark. 1997)

Sabers v. Delano, 100 F. 3d 82 (8th Cir. 1996)

Stumes v. Bloomberg, 551 N.W. 2d 590 (SD 1996)

Tighe v. Wall, 100 F. 3d 41 (5th Cir. 1996)

Tokar v. Armontrout, 97 F. 3d 1078 (8th Cir. 1996)

Tucker v. Graves, 107 F. 3d 881 (10th Cir. 1997)

Turner v. Safley, 482 U.S. 78 (1987)

Washington v. Meachum, 680 A.2d 262 (Conn. 1996)

Williams v. Department of Justice, 433 F. 2d 958 (5th Cir. 1970)

Wolfe v. McDonnell, 418 U.S. 539 (1974)

Women Prisoners of the District of Columbia v. District of Columbia, 93 F. 3d 910 (D.C. Cir. 1996)

Yahweh v. Zavaras, No. 95-1515, 1996 WL 734652 (10th Cir. December 23, 1996)

Younger v. Gilmore, 404 U.S. 15 (1971)

Chapter 3

Impact of the Prison
Litigation Reform Act

Access to the courts has been a continuing issue for the correctional administrator. The primary interest of most inmates has been the appeal of their cases. That is, most inmates seek access to the courts in an attempt to gain their release by challenging their convictions or their sentences. The legal system is structured such that only skilled practitioners can successfully mount a legal challenge. Access to the courts for all, however, is a fundamental value in our society. Thus, unwise litigants who choose to represent themselves are not barred from the attempt. Access to skilled professionals is usually denied to inmates because of their financial status. Most inmates lack the resources to hire a private attorney to pursue their interests. Historically, the primary issue in access has been access to the courts to challenge a petitioner's incarceration. Early litigation focused on matters such as access to legal materials to prepare appeals and on the use of unqualified consultants, prison inmates who have acquired some skill at preparing legal documents but who no formal legal training and who are not members of the bar, the "jailhouse lawyer."

The Prison Litigation
Reform Act of 1995

In response to public outcry surrounding inmate lawsuits about the brand of shoes they are issued by the state or the size of the piece of cake they get for dessert, Congress in 1995 passed the Prison Litigation Reform Act (PLRA), codified at 18 U.S.C. § 3626. In short, the PLRA limits an inmate's access to judicial review of his alleged deprivation of a particular right flowing from a condition of confinement; however, the inmate is still allowed the opportunity to present his grievance.

The Act requires federal courts to give "substantial weight" to the effect that a remedy in favor of an inmate may have on the "public safety or the operation of the criminal justice system" (18 U.S.C. § 3626(a)(1)(A)). The Act also proscribes that any temporary relief afforded a complaining inmate by a court must be "narrowly drawn" and of the means that is least intrusive to the operation of the prison (18 U.S.C. § 3626(a)(2)). The Act prohibits a judicial authority from releasing an inmate from confinement unless a prior least intrusive order has been entered; correctional authorities have failed to correct the problem; and, the offending institution and its administration have had an adequate opportunity to implement the original order (18 U.S.C. § 3626(a)(3)(A)(i-ii)). An order to release a prisoner due to the fact that a problem has not been remedied can only be authorized by a three-judge panel and then only if overcrowding is the root cause of the deprivation. No other relief will remedy the deprivation of the right. (18 U.S.C. § 3626(a)(3)(C-E)).

Once an order of relief is entered, such relief can terminate on motion of either party or an appropriate intervenor two years after the order of relief is entered or one year after the court has denied a previous request to terminate the relief (18 U.S.C. § 3626(b)(1)(A)(i-iii)). If the relief ordered was not, at the time of the entry of the order, determined to be the least intrusive and narrowly drawn for the particular situation, the prison or other entity has a right to an immediate termination of such relief (18 U.S.C. § 3626(b)(1)(B)).

With regard to settlements and consent decrees, once common between correctional administrators and civil libertarian organizations, the PLRA places new and severe restrictions on such arrangements. Now, consent decrees entered by federal courts with regard to institutional conditions must comply with the least intrusive means and narrowly drawn requirements of 18 U.S.C. § 3626(a)(1). No longer can a federal judge strong-arm a prison into what have proven, in some instances, to be crippling agreements with regard to effective and efficient administration of prisons. Such decrees must be directed toward a specific problem. When a prison or other party files for relief from a consent decree, a stay goes into effect thirty days after the filing of the motion for relief, thus eliminating the need for compliance with the decree (18 U.S.C. § 3626(e)(2)(A)(i)).[1] The automatic stay may be postponed for up to sixty days for "good cause," which does not include a congested court calendar (18 U.S.C. § 3626(e)(3)).

Some have argued that the PLRA amounts to a violation of the constitutional doctrine of separation of powers in that the Congress encroached on the judicial power with this legislation, especially with the very strict regulations the legislation places on consent decrees. Costa (1997) asserts that Congress' zealousness to halt alleged litigious prisoners with the PLRA has resulted in virtual elimination of the consent decree as a means for inmates to have their grievances addressed. Additionally, Costa (1997) urges that the PLRA's broad restrictions on the consent decree fail to distinguish between those institutional administrators who enter such agreement for real fiscal and legitimate policy reasons as opposed to those who seek to run wholly unconstitutional institutions. Bloom (1998) contends that the PLRA allows federal, state, and local executive officials to escape their constitutional duties in the operation of correctional facilities by simply alleging that a remedy is not the least intrusive means available. Kuzinski (1998), however, maintains that the real victims in this PLRA struggle are the prison administrators and other political officers, who are forced to defend the most illegitimate claims of constitu-

---

1. In the case where the basis for the filing for relief is based on any other law, the stay beging one hundred and eighty days after the motion is filed. 18 U.S.C. § 3626(e)(2)(A)(ii).

tional shortcomings filed by inmates while fearing that some federal judge will try his or her hand at institutional administration from some courtroom outside the prison boundaries. Bloom (1998) and Decker (1997) expand on the Costa (1997) idea, arguing that the consent decree as an attractive means of resolving prison reform litigation is eliminated because of the restrictions on consent decrees and the fact that consent decrees can be eliminated very easily for failing to comply to the strict dictates of the PLRA.

The Effect of the PLRA on Inmate Claims and Prison Administration

Having provided a preliminary background on the PLRA, it is appropriate to now look at a selection of cases that have been decided since the PLRA became law. While the greater majority of claims under the statute have been disposed of against the complaining inmate, there are cases where the PLRA has not worked to the prisoner's detriment. In *Craig v. Eberly* (1998), a federal appeals court held in favor of an inmate who challenged the retroactive application of the PLRA in his case. The district court below has applied the Act to the inmate's claim regarding constitutional deprivations he suffered as a pre-trial detainee. The appeals court made clear that the PLRA could not be applied retroactively in this context. (See also *Swan v. Banks*, 1998; *Gibbs v. Ryan*, 1998; *Ramsey v. Coughlin*, 1996; *Glover v. Johnson*, 1998 (regarding non-retroactive application of PLRA to attorney's fees)). In addition to the non-retroactive application to cases pending at the time of the enactment of the legislation, courts have also found that the PLRA is applicable to juvenile detention facilities *Alexander S. v. Harpootlian* (1997).

The Fourth Circuit Court of Appeals has declared that the PLRA does not unduly restrict inmates' access to the court nor does the statute violate equal protection principles (*Roller v. Gunn*, 1997), and the Second and Eighth Circuit Courts of Appeals have determined that the PLRA does not violate the separation of powers doctrine with regard to the consent decree termination provision (*Benjamin v. Jacobson*, 1997; *Tyler v. Murphy*, 135 F. 3d 594, 1998).

Alternatives to Litigation

The primary impact of the PLRA is to encourage state and local correctional staff to develop alternatives to litigation. Allen and Simonsen (1998) identify four alternatives to litigation: the grievance board, the inmate grievance procedure, the ombudsman, and mediation.

The typical grievance board is a group of institutional staff that, in some cases, will include representation from the broader community and that is charged with hearing and investigating complaints from inmates. Perhaps its most effective action is to address legitimate inmate complaints early in the process. The board conducts an investigation into each complaint and proposes solutions to correctional staff. If correctional staff accept these recommendations (recommendations are usually not binding on staff) and implement adequate reforms, the inmate's grievance is effectively addressed and his or her cause of action is eliminated. If the staff fail to implement the recommendations, the inmate can continue to assert his or her right to a hearing on the grievance. Of course the inmate's case is strengthened by the finding of the grievance board so staff who ignore board recommendations are at increased risk. If the grievance board finds that there is no merit to the inmate's complaint, the inmate can still pursue his issue but the system now has a fairly complete record of the complaint and can demonstrate that a good faith attempt was made to resolve the issue.

The inmate grievance committee operates just like the grievance board. The primary difference lies in the presence of inmates on the committee. The procedures and outcomes are the same given that there is considerable variation among approaches to the use of the grievance board. The use of inmates as board members gives legitimacy to the process both among inmates and to external reviewers of board actions. Many correctional officials, however, are hesitant to use inmate grievance committees for several reasons: inmates who serve on the committees might gain power in the institution that could be used to frustrate the efforts of the officers to maintain control; inmates might use their positions on the committee to intimidate or control other inmates; and, inmates on the committee might be subject to pressure from inmates who file grievances.

Ombudsman programs vary greatly in implementation. In some cases, the ombudsman is a correctional employee or an employee of another state agency. In others, the ombudsman is an independent contractor or is sponsored by a private non-profit agency. In all cases, the ombudsman represents the inmates. He or she is an inmate advocate and seeks to see to it that the inmate grievance receives a fair hearing. In all cases, the ombudsman is independent of the local manager, usually a warden, reporting to the warden regarding recommendations but administratively responsible to someone outside of the institution. The ombudsman normally has access to all parts of the institution and to all records. In some cases, he or she can pursue issues on his or her own initiative and can investigate an issue without a formal complaint.

Third party mediation is usually conducted by trained mediators who are not directly connected with the department of corrections. Unlike the three other alternatives, mediation tends to be binding on both parties. In other approaches, the warden receives recommendations from the committee or ombudsman and can adopt, modify, or ignore those recommendations. In most cases, the warden must justify any decision to disregard the recommendations and his decision is subject to administrative review and reversal. In mediation the warden or the administrative representative agrees to abide by the mediators' decision before the process begins. It should be noted, however, that mediators are trained to help the confronting parties reach consensus on the issue rather then simply render a decision based on their assessment of the facts in the case.

The goal of all of these programs is to establish a local process that will allow an effective alternative to litigation for inmate complainants. By doing this, systems reduce the number of complaints that move on to the courts and improve the potential for a successful outcome if the case does go to court. If these programs are to be successful, they must be conducted as legitimate activities. That is, if an inmate's complaint is well founded, the validity of the claim must be recognized and effectively addressed. To most correctional administrators, this means reduced control of the institutional environment, an unacceptable position at best. The potential to reduce stress in the environment and reduce the amount of litigation flowing from the facility usually outweighs that loss of control.

The effective removal of the consent decree as a resolution by restricting the conditions under which a consent decree could be entered and limiting the potential scope of consent decrees may have a broader impact than anticipated. By discouraging new consent decrees, the statute brings pressure to bear on existing consent decrees that place restrictions on correctional authorities. It is probable that action will be taken to set aside these agreements by many of those who are presently bound by a restrictive consent decree.

Summary

The federal PLRA was enacted after nearly four decades of increasing inmate litigation, much of which was perceived to be frivolous. It was designed to discourage inmate litigation by making it less likely that inmates would receive favorable outcomes (or at least reduce the degree of favorableness of the outcome) and, while not preventing access, reducing access of inmates to the court. In addition, the Act encouraged the development of alternatives to litigation.

Most correctional systems have implemented a system designed to facilitate effective local resolution of justified complaints filed by inmates. The four alternatives that have emerged include grievance boards, inmate grievance committees, ombudsmen systems, and mediation. By resolving legitimate inmate complaints at the local level, litigation is avoided. By offering a fair hearing, frivolous complaints can be discouraged and, if the inmate chooses to pursue the complaint, he or she has a heavier burden to overcome. A fair hearing has been offered and the authorities have built a sound defense though the resolution process. It is probable that this legislation will encourage challenges to existing consent decrees.

References

Allen, H.E., & Simonsen, C.E. (1998). *Corrections in America.* Upper Saddle River, Prentice Hall, Inc.

Bloom, I. (1998). Prisons, prisoners, and pine forests: Congress breaches the wall separating legislative from judicial power. *Arizona Law Review, 40,* 389-424.

Costa, R.J. (1997). The Prison Litigation Reform Act of 1995: A legitimate attempt to curtail frivolous inmate lawsuits and end the alleged micro-management of state prisons or a violation of separation of powers? *Brooklyn Law Review, 63,* 319-366.

Decker, D. (1997). Consent decrees and the Prison Litigation Reform Act of 1995: Usurping judicial power or quelling judicial micro-management? *Wisconsin Law Review, 1997,* 1275-1321.

Kuzinski, E.J. (1998). The end of the prison law firm? Frivolous inmate litigation, judicial oversight, and the Prison Litigation Reform Act of 1995. *Rutgers Law Journal, 29,* 361-399.

Cases

Alexander S. v. Harpootlian, 113 F. 3d 1373 (4th Cir. 1997)

Benjamin v. Jacobson, 124 F. 3d 162 (2nd Cir. 1997) (modified in 172 F. 3d 144, (2d Cir. 1999))

Craig v. Eberly, 164 F. 3d 490 (10th Cir. 1998)

Gibbs v. Ryan, 160 F. 3d 160 (3rd Cir. 1998)

Glover v. Johnson, 138 F. 3d 229 (6th Cir. 1998)

Ramsey v. Coughlin, 94 F. 3d 71 (2nd Cir. 1996)

Roller v. Gunn, 107 F. 3d 227 (4th Cir. 1997)

Swan v. Banks, 160 F. 3d 1258 (9th Cir. 1998)

Tyler v. Murphy, 135 F. 3d 594 (8th Cir.1998)

Chapter 4

Freedom of Religion

Rehabilitation through religious conversion has been a fundamental element of prisons throughout Western history. Early responses, usually harsh punishments, often blended the interests of the victim, the state, and the church. Punishments were intended to atone to a Supreme Being as well as to the victim and the state. Punishments were intended to help the offender repent and be redeemed (Allen & Simonsen, 1992). In the Middle Ages detention as a means of disposition of the case was the province of the church. In the custom of sanctuary or asylum, the offender was placed in seclusion to reflect and seek penitence. This form of imprisonment became formalized in monasteries and abbeys including long periods of solitary confinement (Allen & Simonsen, 1992). The use of long-term confinement as a disposition in the United States was developed by the Quakers. The Quakers believed that periods of confinement would allow the offender to reflect on his misdeeds and biblical teachings and become penitent or reformed (McKelvey, 1977).

Religion has been an integral part of corrections in the United States throughout its history. Religion is one of the most neglected topics in corrections. Except for an occasional reference to things such as the Quakers and their penitentiary and notation of the delivery of sermons to captive populations by notable religious leaders, few scholars address the issue of religion in the justice system. Religious services are routine in facilities which hold accused and convicted offenders. Religious conversion or recommitment has been seen as a primary form of rehabilitation by every generation. At the same time, religious conversion has never been held in high esteem by correctional managers who tend to question the legitimacy of the conversion of any inmate who hopes to earn eventual release from his or her sentence. All prisons have spaces designated for religious worship and all inmates, regardless of the severity of their behavior, are deemed eligible for religious ministering if they want to express their religious beliefs.

While there are a limited number of paid chaplains, most religious services are provided by volunteers. While the variety of services is substantial, there are four common models for delivery of religious services. One of the most common forms of delivery is the delivery of regular religious service by church groups. A local church will come to the prison on a regular basis and conduct a relatively normal Sunday or weekday evening service. These groups are typically Protestant and provide services that may be attended by inmates of several different Protestant denominations. In some instances, similar programs are offered by Native American, Catholic, Jewish, or Muslim religious groups.

The Protestants also tend to dominate a second form of service-church groups who provide holiday celebrations. These activities generally combine religious services with feasting. The church based group provides food and gifts usually for Easter and Christmas celebrations. Occasionally these groups will provide activities for secular holidays such as the Fourth of July.

The most common form of services is provided by jailhouse preachers. These men and women visit prisons as individuals and provide a full range of religious services including individual counseling. One of the contradictions of religion and corrections is the low regard with which these individuals are held by line officers in an institution which has consistently stressed the need for religious education as a method of reformation. It should be noted that each jailhouse preacher has a set of success stories—men and women whom he or she has helped become successful well-adjusted citizens. We will address the issues that are related to this lack of regard shortly. Jewish and Catholic services tend to be provided by priests and rabbis while Protestant and Muslim services tend to be provided by lay ministers. Counseling has been provided by lay persons from all denominations. The fourth form of delivery of services is though independent non-profit rehabilitation programs. For example, Alabama Volunteers in Corrections (AVIC) was developed by the Alabama Department of Corrections to facilitate the use of volunteers in correctional facilities and programs. While AVIC is a secular program, the volunteers tend to be religious people motivated by religious ideals. It is non-denominational with Jewish, Catholic, Muslim, and Protestant members. It is organized in local chapters, some of which are less non-denominational than others. While secular, the religious agenda is an important part of many of the services provided.

In contrast, Prison Fellowship is a national proselytizing organization. It is fundamental Protestantism at its strongest. Prison Fellowship works with born-again Christians. They provide a full range of services including religious and ministerial training and strong community support on release. Muslim organizations also provide strong community support but lack a specific prison oriented national or state organization. Muslim congregations form in specific prisons then establish links with Muslim congregations in local communities. Men and women are accepted and supported by the local congregations on their release if they continue to adhere to Muslim principles.

Administrative Problems

There are three general concerns in the introduction of any type of volunteer (outsider) into the correctional environment, particularly medium and maximum-security facilities. First, employees fear that volunteers will be deceived by the inmates. Most inmates develop sophisticated manipulation skills that they will use to their own benefit and to the detriment of the prison. Corrections professionals believe that only those who work in corrections can understand and resist inmate attempts to manage their environment. It is assumed that inmates will use false conversions as one manipulative technique to gain support from jailhouse ministers and members of church groups who are seen as being particularly naive because they are very religious. They fear that inmates may misrepresent prison conditions (which are depressing and inhospitable at best) and turn the volunteers against the prison managers.

Any outsider who passes through the security perimeter is a threat to security. Volunteers can unwittingly introduce contraband into the prison environment because they do not know the uses to which inmates may put some objects that appear to be relatively harmless. They can compromise procedures regarding movement and procedures for securing specific areas by simply being in places where they are not expected and by wandering into areas which are restricted all with the best intentions. Staff anxiety is increased when staff suspect that inmates are manipulating volunteers to introduce breaches in security.

Correctional staff need to control the correctional environment. Even well-trained volunteers can compromise the ability of staff to control the environment. Staff are hesitant to move aggressively to control small breaches of institutional rules when "company" is present. Inmates can use these small breaches to irritate staff and to compromise security.

Legal Challenges

Religious freedom was not seriously challenged until the 1970s. Volunteers would enter the prison and either be closely controlled by staff or become informed about proper institutional etiquette and gain limited acceptance by the inmates and the staff. Services provided were predominately Protestant or

Catholic depending on the geographical setting with the chaplain preparing him or herself to meet the needs of inmates of different faiths. Early controversies were satisfied by arranging the chapel or religious space so that it could be converted from a Catholic to a Protestant setup fairly easily.

When the inmate rights movement gained strength in the 1960s, religion became an issue. The freedom of religious practice challenge was fairly complicated, as the fundamental issue is not religion but control. American prisons have been Christian, predominately Protestant. When Americans of African descent began to convert to Islam and form congregations in the prisons, the stage was set for conflict over control of the institution. The needs of Christian inmates were incorporated in the operations and procedures of the prison. Muslims needed changes in the policies and routines of the prison to observe the principles of their faith. These changes included alterations in diet, recognition of new religious holidays, and scheduling of religious services at times consistent with the traditions of the religion practiced by the inmates rather than consistent with contemporary mainstream Protestant traditions. In the 1960s and 1970s, Black Muslim groups, unlike other Muslim groups, were assertively anti-white. Prison congregations wanted their services to be supervised by black officers not white officers. As noted earlier, correctional staff are, at best, skeptical of prison conversions. This skepticism led them to suspect that these groups were more concerned with manipulating their environment than in adhering to clearly held religious beliefs with the issue of race complicating the process. The issue became how much the correctional staff had to change normal operating procedures to accommodate the needs of religious groups. Once the Muslims established their rights, others asserted rights. Some of these new religions were not legitimate; but the legal challenges still tended to be based on the burden the religious regulations placed on correctional staff.

The Non-Impact of the
Religious Freedom Restoration Act
on Religion Behind the Walls

As mentioned in Chapter 1, inmates' individual rights have evolved over time from almost non-existent individual liberty prior to the breach of the hands-off doctrine to a significant increase in rights in the years immediately following the breach. Today there is a public outcry to again limit prisoners' freedoms behind the walls. One highly litigated area of prisoners' liberty has come in the area of religion and religious practice.

In 1987, the U.S. Supreme Court decided a New Jersey case brought by inmates who were members of the Islamic faith challenging institutional restrictions on their religious practices (*O'Lone v. Estate of Shabazz, et al.,* 1987). Specifically, the plaintiffs in *O'Lone* alleged that the prison work policy prevented them from freely exercising their faith by attending Jumu'ah, a Friday afternoon prayer service. The work policy required inmates to vacate their buildings for various work assignments and prohibited them from reentering those buildings until day's end; thus, the prayer service could not be attended. The federal district court found that no constitutional violation occurred, as the prison policies were consistent with the ideals of security, order, and rehabilitation. The U.S. Court of Appeals for the Third Circuit reversed the district court, finding that the institutional policies restricting the prisoners' free exercise claims were constitutionally firm only if the State of New Jersey's prison authority demonstrated that the restrictions served the interests of order and security and "...that no reasonable method exists by which [prisoners'] religious rights can be accommodated without creating bona fide security problems" (*Shabazz v. O'Lone,* 1986, p. 420).

New Jersey sought relief from the U.S. Supreme Court. The appeal was taken up by the Court, which reversed the Third Circuit. Writing for the 5-4 majority, Chief Justice William Rehnquist found that the burden placed on prison officials was to demonstrate that no accommodation existed which would not result in a security breach: "[t]hough the availability of accommodations is relevant to the reasonableness inquiry, we have rejected the notion..." that prison administrators must address every possible way of providing an inmate accommodations for alleged infringements of constitutional rights (*O'Lone v. Estate of Shabazz, et al.*, 1987, p. 350).

As Rachanow (1998) notes "[t]he O'Lone court adopted a new, less stringent test for judging prisoner' free exercise claims...." (p. 126). This case, however, was the second of the Court's 1986-87 term where broader authority to institutional administrators was affirmed. In *Turner v. Safley* (1987), decided eight days before *O'Lone*, the Court held that the reasonableness test applied to inmate correspondence restrictions and inmate marriage relations. So long as the prison regulations reasonably relate to specific and legitimate penological goals then such regulations are constitutionally valid (*Turner v. Safley*, 1987).

Thus, the *O'Lone* reasonableness standard applied to all inmate free exercise claims. The scope of an inmate's free exercise of religion could be limited or even eliminated under the *O'Lone* standard provided that prison administrators could identify a legitimate penological interest in the restriction.

Following the U.S. Supreme Court's decision in *Employment Division, et al. v. Smith* (1990), however, a non-prison case, the U.S. Congress was disturbed and moved to enact legislation aimed at what was seen as a intrusion on individual religious liberty. In *Smith*, the Court ruled that the State of Oregon could deny state benefits to individuals fired from their jobs for using ceremonial peyote despite the claims of the employees that the use was for religious purposes. The Court held that a generally applicable criminal law that is not aimed at religious discrimination cannot be avoided by a claim of religious freedom. As Chemerinsky (1998) notes, the *Smith* decision "...changed the law of the Free Exercise Clause dramatically" (p. 629). In short, despite the burden that a generally applicable criminal law may place on one's religious practice, the burden is appropriate as long as the law was not "...motivated by a desire to interfere with religion" (Chemerinsky, 1998, p. 630).

The Religious Freedom Restoration Act of 1993 (RFRA) passed Congress with broad bipartisan support. In sum, the RFRA decreed:

> Government shall not substantially burden a person's exercise of religion even if the burden results from a rule of general applicability.... (42 U.S.C. § 2000bb-1(a) (1993))

The RFRA provided two exceptions to the rule above where there was a compelling government interest and where there was such an interest, the least restrictive means was employed to further that interest (42 U.S.C. § 2000bb-1(b) (1993)). The administrative effect of the RFRA on prisons and jails was a prominent part of the floor debates and legislative history of this bill. With regard to correctional institutions, the legislative history specifically notes that courts were expected to continue to give "...due deference to the experience and expertise..." of wardens and other administrators in establishing appropriate rules to guarantee order and security in jails and prisons (1993 U.S.C.A.N. 1892, 1900). Thus, as Laycock and Thomas (1994) observed, it seems that Congress was very concerned with the RFRA applying in context. While this observation is true, it also appears that while Congress was concerned with the context in which the RFRA would apply, legislators also intended for prison administrators to demonstrate a real threat, much like the requirement of the Third Circuit Court of Appeals in *Shabazz v. O'Lone* (1986), as the Supreme Court's decision in *O'Lone* is referenced in the legislative history of the RFRA as having chilled inmate' religious practices.

Abbott (1995) notes that the RFRA prompted much concern from state and local law enforcement, from attorneys general to prison wardens, who viewed the legislation as a real threat to the safe, secure, and orderly operation of correctional facilities. The RFRA, however, did not have a serious positive impact on inmates' religious claims. While a few cases granted the relief sought based on the RFRA, the majority of cases continued to apply the *O'Lone* reasonableness standard. As Solove (1996) points out, judges were leery of applying the RFRA to inmate claims because of their lack of expertise in prison management. Judges, it seems, feared that their application of the RFRA might adversely impact order and discipline behind the walls.

Thus, the declaration of the RFRA as being unconstitutional in 1997 (*City of Boerne v. Flores*) did not have a major effect on inmates' claims of freedom of religion violations. As noted above, the *O'Lone* reasonableness standard was applied by many courts even while the RFRA was in effect.

Summary

Religion has been an affirmative integral part of American prisons since their inception. Regardless of the general public attitude toward the disposition of criminal offenders in effect at the time, religious practice leading to religious conversion or reaffirmation have been accepted as a legitimate process in the correctional environment. All correctional administrators identify space that can be devoted to observance of religious rituals and most provide a paid chaplain to minister to the religious needs of those inmates who choose to maintain or attempt to regain their faith. Christianity, predominately Protestant Christianity, has dominated correctional religious services with most religious services provided by volunteers, both professional and lay religious people.

The rise of the practice of Islam among Americans of African descent coincided with the movement to protect basic inmates' rights giving rise to challenges to Christian-oriented rules and procedures which restricted the ability of Muslims to properly obey the proscriptions of their religion. Control of the institution was an underlying issue with many correctional officers and managers suspecting that the inmates were attempting to manipulate their environment more then they were attempting to respect the rules of their new religious beliefs.

Litigation has focused on the legitimacy of the security issues generally argued as a reason for enforcing rather than modifying correctional rules and procedures. This issue may become moot as most prisons have discovered that the presence of a strong Muslim community tends to act as a stabilizing force in the prison. That is, both devout Christians and devote Muslims are oriented toward leading a lawful life and begin by being less troublesome in the correctional environment. Many correctional administrators accommodate and facilitate the development and practice of any legitimate religious activity.

References

Abbott, C. (1995). Dam the RFRA at the prison gate: The Religious Freedom Restoration Act's impact on correctional litigation. *Montana Law Review, 56,* 325-347.

Allen, H.E., & Simonsen, C.E. (1992). *Corrections in America.* New York: Macmillan.

Chemerinsky, E. (1998). The Religious Freedom Restoration Act is a constitutional expansion of rights. *William and Mary Law Review, 39,* 601-636.

Laycock, D., & Thomas, O.S. (1994). Interpreting the Religious Freedom Restoration Act. *Texas Law Review, 73,* 209-245.

McKelvey, B. (1977). *American prisons: A history of good intentions.* Montclair, NJ: Patterson Smith Publishing Company.

Rachanow, S.S. (1998). The effect of *O'Lone v. Estate of Shabazz* on the free exercise rights of prisoners. *Journal of Church and State, 40,* 125-149.

Religious Freedom Restoration Act of 1993, Pub. L. No. 103-141, 107 Stat. 1488, 1993 U.S.C.A.N. 1892, codified at 42 U.S.C. § 2000bb, et seq. (1993).

Solove, D.J. (1996). Faith profaned: The Religious Freedom Restoration Act and religion in prisons. *Yale Law Journal, 106,* 459-491.

Cases

City of Boerne v. Flores , 521 U.S. 507 (1997)

Employment Division, Department of Human Resources of Oregon v. Smith, 494 U.S. 872 (1990)

O'Lone v. Estate of Shabazz, et al., 482 U.S. 342 (1987)

Shabazz v. O'Lone, 782 F. 2d 416 (3d Cir. 1986)

Turner v. Safley, 482 U.S. 78 (1987)

Chapter 5

Impact of
Sentencing Reform

The purpose of sentencing has been controversial throughout the history of criminal justice. Early development of corrections in the United States was motivated by adding alternatives to what were perceived at the time to be unacceptable dispositions in cases in which defendants were found guilty. The Quakers were attempting to develop a new type of sentencing which would enable rehabilitation through penitence when they instituted the first penitentiary unit in the old Walnut Street Jail and later in the penitentiaries which were modeled on the Pennsylvania system (McKelvey, 1977). The correctional institution was one form of early sentencing reform.

While there are various schemes presented to explain sentencing, five functions or goals of sentencing have been advanced: deterrence, incapacitation, punishment, rehabilitation, and restitution. In most cases, the sentence is presumed to serve more than one function. The issue is complicated by the fact that most specific sentences which include incarceration can be argued to serve any one or all of the functions. A sentence to a correctional institution can serve as deterrence both to the offender and to those who are aware of the disposition of the case. The same sentence can serve to protect the public by removing the risk posed by the offender for the period of the sentence. It can punish by depriving the offender of his or her personal freedom and by placing the offender in an unpleasant environment. It can be argued that incarceration can produce rehabilitation by providing the offender with an opportunity to reflect on the consequences of criminal behavior and through access to counseling, educational, and training programs. It can also be argued that the same sentence enables the payment of restitution if the offender is placed in a work release program. The issue is not so much what we do as the reason that we say that we do it.

Contemporary arguments as to why we sentence, however, have produced sentencing reforms that directly impact on the operation of correctional facilities. Underlying this debate is a belief by advocates on both sides of the issue that sentencing should reduce criminal behavior. While five functions have been identified, the debate focuses on two, rehabilitation versus punishment or just deserts. These two different perspectives are based in two long-standing theories of disposition of criminal offenders, the classical school and the positive school.

The classical school also produced an early sentencing reform movement. The classical school emerged during the Eighteenth Century period of Enlightenment and challenged what appeared to be an irrational sentencing process in which the sentence which a criminal offender received was not necessarily related to the act for which he or she was convicted or to the characteristics of the offender. Punishments were seen as both inhuman and inequitable (Abadinsky, 1997). Classical school scholars place sentencing in the context of both the rational man perspective and the social contract perspective produced during the Enlightenment. From this perspective, offenders commit crimes because they choose to do so. As rational beings, they are motivated by the rewarding consequences of their behaviors. Punishment should be designed to outweigh the pleasure the offender receives from the criminal act. Punishments should be determined by the nature of the crime and should only be severe enough to deter future acts. These sentences should be uniformly applied to all offenders regardless of rank and should be clearly established in the codified law (Maestro, 1973). From the classical school perspective, the sentence should be based on the nature of the crime rather than the nature of the criminal.

The positive school emerged in the Eighteenth Century and reflected a move to the application of scientific methods to understanding criminal behavior and the emergence of the discipline of criminology. Lombroso (1911) argued that criminal behavior has a physiological basis. While the concept of the atavistic personality did not prevail, the deterministic perspective underlying his model did. From the deterministic perspective, the offender is not responsible for his or her behavior. Criminal behavior is caused by a physiological condition or a mental condition beyond the offender's control or, in later theories, by socialization into specific roles determined by the offender's environment or by the social structure in which he or she is located. If the offender is not responsible for his or her criminal behavior, punishment is not an appropriate response. Convicted offenders should be treated or rehabilitated (Abadinsky, 1997). From the classical perspective, the sentence should be based on the nature of the criminal rather than on the nature of the crime. In the United States, the system tends to cycle from the classical to the positive perspective as a basis for determining the appropriate disposition for convicted criminal offenders. It should also be noted that the initiation of a new cycle, whether classical or positive, tends to produce a period of longer sentences for selected classes of offenders. During classical dominated periods, determinate sentences are preferred and all sentences tend to become longer. During positive periods, the indeterminate sentence is preferred which permits offenders non-amenable to treatment to be incarcerated for longer periods of time than offenders amenable to treatment.

The rehabilitation ideal is believed to have dominated corrections throughout the Nineteenth Century and most of the Twentieth Century (Allen, 1981). The alternating preference for punishment or treatment pre-dates the use of the prison as a sentence. Shifts in the cycle from treatment to punishment can be seen in the development of the workhouse or the development of the English Poor Laws. The development of the prison as a disposition in the late 1600s was the product of a sentencing reform movement that sought to reduce crime through the treatment of criminal offenders and was to replace less humane dispositions, such as corporal punishment and capital punishment. By the early 1700s, sentiment had changed and, while the prison was maintained, the colonial assembly re-imposed the English criminal code, including capital punishment and whipping (McKelvey, 1977).

Clear peaks in the cycles are difficult to identify during the 1800s because of the different rates of development of prison systems in the various states (Morgan & Sigler, 1998). While some states had well established systems which progressed through stages of development and reform, other states did not build prisons until the latter part of the century (McKelvey, 1977). In those states with well-developed systems, pressure for reform in the disposition of offenders began to emerge in the early 1800s. This pressure produced the use of indeterminate sentences, prison societies, probation and parole, and the reformatory movement with firm discipline and education defined as part of the treatment process (McKelvey, 1977). By the end of the 1800s, the cycle was shifting, as reflected in statutes providing for longer sentences for minor offenders, the use of some mandatory sentences, habitual offender statutes, restrictions on the use of parole, and statutes criminalizing vagrancy. In the 1930s and 1940s the medical model emerged and classification shifted with an emphasis on classifying inmates for treatment and on an upgrading of the status of parole beginning with the federal system and moving to the states (McKelvey, 1977). Legislation and practice emerged permitting the implementation and expansion of the medical model of treatment, including enabling statutes, modified death penalty statutes, and the expanded good time provisions (McKelvey, 1977).

By the 1970s sentiment had shifted away from treatment. Rehabilitation was perceived as a failure with the severity of crime perceived as increasing and the safety of the public decreasing because of the emphasis on treatment in the correctional system (Allen, 1981; Fogel, 1978). Reformers who advocated punishment as the correct function of sentencing prevailed, and incarceration became prominent. Legislative initiatives restored determinate sentences, abolished parole, reestablished or strengthened habitual offender provisions, increased the use of sentence enhancement, and developed sentencing guidelines. As a result, the incarceration rate more than doubled between 1973 and 1983 (Currie, 1985). This trend has continued and, presently, correctional systems are unable to house all of those sentenced to state incarceration, in spite of aggressive construction programs (Morgan & Sigler, 1998). For example, Mississippi, despite aggressive prison construction over the last several years, was faced with a May 2000 federal court madate to deal with continued overcrowding problems related to the housing of inmates in county jails.

Contemporary Practices

Punishment presently dominates policy, legislation, and practice regarding convicted offenders. Society is moving toward dependence upon punishment to deter criminals from criminal activity (Morgan & Sigler, 1998). Contemporary shifts toward punishment are often characterized as in the classical tradition however, the development of severe penalties violates the proportionality provision of the classical school and the permanent incapacitation statutes tend to be more in the positive tradition than the classical tradition (permanent incapacitation of the untreatable offender). Contemporary sentence reform tends to reflect retribution rather than the classical school's deterrence through measured punishment approach.

Three types of legislative initiatives reflect a shift in orientation toward punishment: habitual offender statues, other sentence enhancement alternatives, and determinate sentencing (with a reduction/elimination of the use of parole). These statutes are enacted to control dangerous or. serious criminal offenders. An increase in public safety through the use of incarceration to control severe offenders is characteristic of periods in which punishment dominates disposition philosophy.

These initiatives developed in the federal system. Sentencing disparity, particularly insufficiently punishing sentences for some offenders, became an important issue for Congress during the 1970s. Congress charged the United States Parole Commission with the task of developing a plan to address the problems involved in sentencing offenders. The plan that was developed was short-lived because of lack of judicial acceptance. The second plan advanced involved rewriting the federal criminal code, but it, too, was not implemented successfully. The third plan focused on sentencing reform and proposed a comprehensive criminal law package, the Comprehensive Crime Control Act of 1984, and included the Sentencing Reform Act (Wilkins, Newton, & Steer, 1993).

The purpose of the Sentencing Reform Act was to enhance the ability of the criminal justice system to combat crime through an effective, fair sentencing system. In order to achieve this goal, Congress identified three objectives: (a) the sentence imposed would be the actual sentence served, except for "good-time" credits, and the possibility of parole would not be a factor; (b) there would be uniformity in sentencing practices; and (c) the sentence would be proportional to the defendant and the offense (Wilkins, Newton, & Steer, 1993). Several states have followed the federal model by enactment of similar sentencing procedures that provide for sentence enhancements for the career criminal. Common characteristics of sentence enhancement statutes are: "(a) imposition of a greater sentence for persons convicted under another statutory provision; (b) procedures for sentence hearings; and (c) titles that classify them as sentence enhancing statutes" (Rafaloff, 1988, p. 1090).

Habitual Offender Statutes

In an attempt to reduce recidivism, many states have enacted habitual offender acts. This is a direct response to evaluations that question the effectiveness of correctional programs in reducing criminality (Maltz, 1984). Maltz concluded that (a) nothing works or is an effective deterrent to reducing recidivism and (b) getting tough works if the intervention is tough enough. States that have enacted habitual offender acts hold the belief that getting tough works. Habitual offender statutes tend to reflect most clearly the preference for incarceration as a disposition. Forty-three states had adopted legislation providing for mandatory sentencing for offenders who demonstrated repeated violations of felony statutes by 1983 (U.S. Department of Justice, 1983). Attempts to understand the "criminal," the individual who earns his or her livelihood by committing criminal acts, have dominated criminology since its inception. Research indicates that as many as 80% (Shinnar & Shinnar, 1975) or 85% (Wolfgang, Figlio, & Sellin, 1972) of serious crimes committed are committed by habitual offenders. Habitual offender acts attempt to control this population by assigning longer sentences to repeat felony offenders.

The indiscriminate use of longer sentences for repeat offenders is not effective because plea bargaining, lack of information, and other factors can and do reduce the judge's freedom in assigning a sentence. The use of automatic sentencing has been present since as early as 1926 (Inciardi, 1986) when legislation very similar to current habitual offender legislation was introduced in the New York Legislature with a mandatory life sentence following a fourth felony conviction. Contemporary proposals for selective incapacitation (Blackmore & Welsh, 1983; Janus, 1985), which are the product of both a desire to control career offenders and pressure to contain the growth of prison populations, are an updated version of an old response to an enduring problem. Attempts to develop an effective operational definition for habitual offenders have led to the reduction of this concept to a specific number of felonies, thus creating a condition in which the offenders captured by the statute may not be the career criminals sought. Relatively non-dangerous offenders could commit three mild felonies (a popular threshold for many legislatures), plead guilty to all three and receive a harsh sentence for a fourth mild felony offense. The career criminal or the individual with a criminal orientation would avoid the statute by bargaining for a plea to a reduced charge (a misdemeanor), by leaving the jurisdiction after posting bond and avoiding a conviction, or by moving from jurisdiction to jurisdiction during his or her criminal career (Morgan & Sigler, 1998).

Sentence Enhancement

Habitual offender acts also have sentence enhancement provisions (add one or more years to the sentence when two or more prior convictions exist) which mandate the use of a life without parole sentence for some (usually on the fourth felony conviction), regardless of the dangerousness or level of commitment to criminal behavior. Other statutes provide for life without parole sentences because of the severity or offensiveness of the act. These statutes permit the assignment of a life without parole sentence when an offender's behavior is so dangerous that society has an interest in incarceration for public safety and/or for punishment. If the statutes are effective, there should be two life without parole populations. One is composed of offenders (who may not be career criminals) who have committed extremely offensive and dangerous acts, usually involving an element of physical assault; the other is a group of career criminals who frequently have no personal violence in their offense history (Morgan & Sigler, 1998). Habitual offenders tend to be the younger, more violent, and more assertive offenders (Flanagan, 1982; Irwin, 1981). If the habitual offender acts are ineffective, a third group of life without parole inmates is created. This group of offenders exhibits relatively mild levels of criminal activity and is not dangerous. Common characteristics of sentence enhancement statutes are: (a) imposition of a greater sentence for persons convicted under another statutory provision; (b) procedures for sentence hearings; and (c) titles that classify them as sentence enhancing statutes (Rafaloff, 1988, p. 1090).

Carrying a weapon during the commission of a crime is the most common type of sentence enhancement statute after habitual offender acts. Many of these statutes automatically impose increasingly severe penalties as the role of the weapon in the offense incident becomes more severe.

Consequences for Corrections

Legislators failed to realize the impact that sentence enhancements would have on prison populations and prison management. Sentence enhancements have contributed greatly to the problem of prison overcrowding in many states. For this reason, many prison officials have reconstructed their programs to accommodate the increase in population. The overall effects of punitive sentence reforms extend beyond the inmate population increase and prison management to include the management of human and material resources (Luttrell, 1991, p. 54).

The growth in prison populations has been attributed to changes in the orientation of the justice system (MacKenzie, Tracy, & Williams, 1988). Prior to 1980, growth in Louisiana prisons was related to demographic changes in the general population, but the rapid growth of Louisiana's prison population in the early 1980s has been attributed to a number of changes in the law which increased the severity of sentences (MacKenzie, Tracy, & Williams, 1988). Similar statutes have been adopted in many states.

The cost of maintaining the life without parole population is high. If the use of these recent, more severe statutes is heavy, a department of corrections might be required to build a new prison every two or three years to accommodate new life without parole offenders. These prisons would be expensive, secure facilities requiring more and better-qualified staff. Thus, in addition to adding the cost of staffing and maintaining new institutions to the operating budget of the department of corrections, the cost per inmate would increase as well.

Summary

As civilization has developed, attempts to deal effectively with those who choose to disobey the rules and laws of their society have evolved. Each reform comes to be defined as uncivilized by future generations and is replaced by a new reform. At times, the new reform is regressive but the trend is toward more effective dispositions in the treatment of criminal offenders. At present, sentencing of criminal offenders is becoming more punishment or deterrence oriented. When the deterrence orientation of the classical perspective dominates, sentences are based on the crime itself rather than on the rehabilitation or treatment needs of the sentence reduction of sentence disparity is important producing responses such as sentencing guidelines. The punitive orientation produces sentencing reform such as sentence enhancements, abolishment of parole, and habitual offender acts. The impact of these changes is increased use of incarceration.

Sentencing reform—particularly strong sentence enhancements, serving full sentences, and the increasingly punitive drug laws—is producing increasingly large prison populations. The growth in prison populations is considerably higher than the number of new beds under construction. As this trend continues, overcrowding will produce many of the same conditions that produced the cases that led to the overturning of the hands-off doctrine. While the present Supreme Court is more conservative than the court that produced substantial reform in the way correctional systems do business, there may be a point at which they will intercede on constitutional grounds.

References

Abadinsky, H. (1997) *Law and justice*. Chicago: Nelson Hall.

Allen, F.A. (1981). *The decline of the rehabilitative ideal: Penal policy and social purpose*. New Haven, CT: Yale University Press.

Blackmore, J., & Welsh, J. (1983). Selective incapacitation: Sentencing according to risk. *Crime and Delinquency, 29*(4), 505-527.

Currie, E. (1985). *Confronting crime*. New York: Pantheon Books.

Flanagan, T. (1982). Correctional policy and the long-term prisoner. *Crime and Delinquency, 28*(1), 82-95.

Fogel, D. (1978). *We are the living proof, 2nd ed*. Cincinnati, OH: Anderson Press.

Inciardi, J.(1986). *Criminal justice*. New York: Harcourt Brace, Jovanovich.

Irwin, D. (1981). Sociological studies of the impact of long-term confinement. In D. Ward & K.F. Schoen (Eds.) *Confinement in Maximum Custody*. Lexington, MA: Lexington Books.

Janus, M. (1985). Selective incapacitation: Have we tried it? Does it work? *Journal of Criminal Justice, 3*, 117-129.

Lombroso, C. (1968). *Crime its causes and remedies*. Montclair, NJ: Patterson Smith (originally published in 1911).

Luttrell, M. (1990). The impact of the sentencing reform act on prison management. *Federal Probation, 55* (4), 54-57.

MacKenzie, D.L., Tracy, G.S., & Williams G. (1988). Incarceration rates and demographic change hypothesis. *Journal of Criminal Justice, 16*(3), 212-253.

McKelvey, B. (1977). *American prisons: A history of good intentions*. Montclair, NJ: Patterson Smith.

Maestro, M. (1973). *Cesare Beccaria and the origins of penal reform*. Philadelphia: Temple University Press.

Maltz, M. (1984). *Recidivism*. Orlando: Academic Press, Inc.

Morgan, E.F. & Sigler, R.T. (1998). Sentencing into the Twenty-First Century: Sentence Enhancement and Life-Without-Parole. In Roslyn Muraskin (Ed.) *Visions for change: Crime and justice in the twenty-first century,* (351-366)(rev.ed.). Singing River, NJ: Prentice Hall.

Rafaloff, J. (1988). The armed career criminal act: Sentence enhancement or new offense? *Fordham Law Review, 56,* 1085-1099.

Shinnar, E., & Shinnar, K. (1975). The effects of the criminal justice system on the control of crime: A qualitative approach. *Law and Society Review, 23*(4), 547.

U.S. Department of Justice (1983). *Setting prison terms.* Washington, DC: Bureau of Justice Statistics.

Wilkins, Jr., W., Newton, P., & Steer, J. (1993). Competing sentencing policies in a "war on drugs" era. *Wake Forest Law Review, 28,* 305-327.

Wolfgang, M., Figlio, M., & Sellin, T. (1972*). Delinquency in a birth cohort.* Chicago: University of Chicago Press.

Chapter 6

Issues in the
Incarceration of
Death Row Inmates

Capital punishment appears to be one of the oldest penalties used by organized groups to enforce compliance to the laws and rules the group establishes for the mutual benefit of the members of the group. It is interesting to note that Beccaria, in the formulation of the classical perspective, was opposed to the use of capital punishment as a sentence. He believed that it was not particularly useful as a deterrent (Hawkins & Alpert, 1989). The use of capital punishment has been an enduring issue in the United States. Debates regarding the appropriateness of capital punishment as a civilized response have been present since the early periods of settlement and the period during which government and legal traditions were established. The debate is conducted by opposing groups with substantial commitments to their respective positions; thus, court challenges have been frequent. Perhaps because it is such a controversial issue, the courts have not always spoken clearly on the issue.

The death penalty was first successfully challenged in the United States in the early 1900s. During that period, the debate led to the abolishment of capital punishment as a sentence for criminal offenders in a number of states. Reform activities were driven by efforts to produce legislation forbidding the use of the penalty rather than by challenges of the legality of the sentence in the judicial system. Since that time, some states have joined the group of states that choose to abstain and others have reestablished the death penalty after a period of abstinence (Carlson & Garrett, 1999). As of 1996, 38 states had legislation in place permitting the use of capital punishment as a sentencing disposition (Deiter, 1999).

The satisfaction of a capital sentence was relatively rapid and effective until the 1960s. Cases brought before the courts in the 1960s that challenged the use of capital punishment on a broad range of issues slowed the speed with which offenders sentenced to death were executed. Advocates of the abolition of the death penalty mustered their resources and pursued every avenue of appeal for inmates on death row. This effort culminated in the *Furman* decision in which the Supreme Court ruled that the inequitable application of the death penalty created a condition of cruel and unusual punishment sufficient to establish a constitutional violation. The 38 states which authorized the use of the death sentence set about the task of crafting legislation which would remove the potential for arbitrary application of the death sentence. In 1976, the Supreme Court approved parts of an act passed by the Georgia State Legislature and the death penalty once more became a viable sentencing option in selected cases (Carlson & Garrett, 1999).

The use of capital punishment is justified by supporters on several principles including retribution, just deserts, and deterrence. While the right of the victim or victim's family to address their grief though state retribution on their behalf and the lack of redeeming value or mitigating circumstances which could be used as a basis for an appeal to reduce punishment in many capital cases are clear and difficult to oppose in most capital cases, deterrence is more frequently argued by proponents of the death penalty. The deterrence argument is complicated and is more than the simple incapacitation function. Proponents argue that executions deter potential offenders in the community and that executions reinforce the contemporary community moral structure.

The use of capital punishment is illegitimatized by opponents on several principles including discrimination or equity and rejection of the effectiveness of deterrence. The discrimination argument was particularly effective as a bar to executions until death penalty states developed legislation that reduced the discriminatory effect of application of the death penalty. Opponents of the death penalty argue that the death penalty increases the likelihood that others in the community will commit violent acts and reduces the contemporary community moral structure. In its simplest form, the argument states that if the state can resolve its issues by killing someone, others will believe that they are justified in using force to resolve their issues. Both opponents and proponents argue that their position is the appropriate moral position.

While most of the litigation has focused on the constitutionality of the use of the death penalty itself, there are a number of issues related to the maintenance of death row inmates and to the nature of the execution itself. The legal status of the death row inmate is an issue. In most states, death row inmates are not state inmates. They have not been sentenced to the department of corrections to serve a specific sentence. Death row inmates are detained by the department of corrections until their sentence can be carried out. In essence, inmates are still held under the jurisdiction of the sentencing court and are county inmates rather than state inmates. One impact of this status is that departments of corrections will not house death row inmates with non-death row inmates. This isolation is enforced to the extent that, in most institutions, when death row inmates are moved within the institution, the other inmates are locked down (locked in their cells) while the death row inmate is moved. The isolation of the death row inmates is based in part on the need to protect the death row inmate and in part on the degree of risk that the death row inmate represents. One of the responsibilities of the correctional staff is to keep the death row inmate alive until his or her execution. Many death row inmates have committed acts that would make them targets of other inmates. That is, some inmates in the general maximum security population would kill a death row inmate, given the opportunity, who had sexually abused and killed young children or who had been particularly sadistic (a criteria for application of the death penalty) in the commission of his criminal acts.

Death row inmates must be kept in maximum security environments because they are likely to attempt suicide, are highly likely to escape if given the opportunity (they have nothing to lose in an escape attempt), and because they are inherently dangerous. Death row inmates are perceived to be more likely to commit suicide than other inmates are. They live in poor conditions at best and have little or no hope of eventual release. Correctional staff have a duty to make a good effort to prevent the death of any inmate. The very acts which have qualified them for the death penalty are the types of acts that cause an inmate to be identified as too dangerous to be held in anything less than a maximum security environment.

Departments of corrections address these issues by holding death row inmates in dedicated high security cellblocks, which minimize their freedom of movement and choice of activities and present, at best, a stark environment. These conditions have led to litigation protesting these conditions.

Death row cellblocks are operated as segregation units. Inmates are locked in their cells for at least 23 hours a day. They are allowed out of their cells for the minimum time needed to permit mandated exercise and to shower. The segregation environment is Spartan at best. Food is served from a central kitchen and is eaten in the cell. The amount and type of personal property allowed in the death row inmate's cell varies greatly from place to place and occasionally from time to time within the same institution. Visits and all forms of communication with the outside community are generally very restricted.

The correctional staff also have to be prepared to manage demonstrators with conflicting positions. Both opponents and proponents travel to the correctional facility to protest as an execution date and time approach. Access to state property can be limited but demonstrators have a right to express their opinion. In many cases, correctional staff seek assistance from the state highway patrol for the management of these groups, and very little litigation has been undertaken to assert the rights of the demonstrators.

There has been some discussion of the rights of correctional employees to dissociate themselves from an execution. That is, can an employee refuse to participate in an execution? This has not become an issue as most correctional administrators will respect an employee's preference in this regard and employees opposed to the death penalty will not be assigned death row duties. An employee with an ethical objection to capital punishment will generally not be compelled to participate; thus, there has been little litigation on this issue.

The manner in which the inmate is executed has been the focus of litigation. The argument is that even if capital punishment is not cruel and unusual per se, certain types of execution are excessively painful. Over the centuries, various governments have devised innovative and particularly painful forms of execution. Present moral standards will not permit the intentional infliction of pain during an execution. Opponents and proponents debate the extent to which the various forms of execution are unnecessarily painful. Each form of execution that has been challenged has been replaced by another form of execution that is then challenged. The firing squad, hanging, electrocution, gas, and injection have all been challenged with graphic examples of the death experience as recorded by witnesses and, at times, captured on videotape.

Litigation and Legislation

The Cruel and Unusual Punishment Clause of the Eighth Amendment was recognized to be fully applicable to the states through the due process clause of the Fourteenth Amendment in *Robinson v. California* 370 U.S. 660 (1962), a case where the appellant Robinson was incarcerated for his status of being a narcotics addict. Once the clause was made fully applicable to the states, challenges to state sentences increased.

One important challenged area of sentencing of constitutional significance lies in the continuing debate over proportionality in sentencing. The main thrust of the proportionality argument centers over sentence lengths for similar offenses and offenders as well as victim profiles as related to offender characteristics. The U.S. Supreme Court considered the proportionality argument in *Solem v. Helm*, 463 U.S. 277 (1983). In *Helm*, the Court announced the important principle of law "that a criminal sentence must be proportionate to the crime for which the defendant has been convicted. Reviewing courts, of course, should grant substantial deference to the broad authority that legislatures necessarily possess in determining the types and limits of punishments for crimes, as well as to the discretion that trial courts possess in sentencing convicted criminals. But no penalty is per se constitutional." *Id.* at 289. The Court went on to establish three factors which must be considered by a trial court before imposing a criminal sanction: the gravity of the offense and the harshness of the penalty, a comparison of the sentences imposed on other criminals in the same jurisdiction, and a comparison of the sentences imposed for commission of the same crime in other jurisdictions. *Id.* 291. In 1991, the Court again reached the issue of proportionality, limiting *Helm* in holding that certain mandatory, lengthy sentences may be cruel, but are not per se unconstitutional (*Harmelin v. Michigan*, 501 U.S. 957, 994 (1991)).

Capital Sentencing

Academic discussion regarding the methods of punishment is no more lively and sincere than in the area of capital punishment. Many cases have come before the U.S. Supreme Court challenging the constitutionality of capital punishment. That jurisprudence has resulted in a period of almost no restrictions, to a total ban, and presently, on increased usage of the ultimate sanction and a public sentiment geared toward imposing the penalty more quickly with fewer appeals. One of the early cases regarding the death penalty was *Wilkerson v. Utah*, 99 U. S. 130 (1878). In that case, Utah law provided that "a person convicted of a capital offense should suffer death by being shot, hanged, or beheaded," as the court might direct, or he should "have his option as to the manner of his execution." Justice Clifford, for the Court, sustained the statute finding no conflict with the statute and the cruel and unusual punishment clause.

Twelve years later, the Court again had occasion to consider the constitutionality of capital punishment in a petition for habeas corpus from a state inmate. Chief Justice Fuller wrote: "Punishments are cruel when they involve torture or a lingering death; but the punishment of death is not cruel, within the meaning of that word as used in the Constitution. It implies there is something inhuman and barbarous, and something more than the mere extinguishment of life" (*In Re Kemmler*, 136 U. S. 436, 447 (1890)). Ultimately, *Klemmer* turned on a jurisdictional question, to which the Court responded that the Eighth Amendment was inapplicable to the states.

As the death penalty was seen by many to be arbitrary in its application, litigation continued to be brought forward, culminating with a series of cases beginning in 1971 that would lead to the temporary halt of capital punishment in America. In *McGautha v. California* and *Crampton v. Ohio* (consolidated at 402 U.S. 183 (1971)), California's practice of allowing juries to impose the death sentence without guidelines and standards and Ohio's practice of allowing a jury to consider guilt and sentence in one trial were found not to offend the protections found in the Constitution.

Only one term later, however, the Supreme Court make a complete turn on the issues presented in *McGautha* and *Crampton*. In *Furman v. Georgia* 408 U.S. 238 (1972), the Court, in nine separate opinions with 5 concurring votes, found that the imposition of the death penalty was unconstitutional under the

Eighth and Fourteenth Amendments, because, in the words of Justice Potter Stewart, the Constitution "cannot tolerate the infliction of a sentence of death under legal systems that permit this unique penalty to be so wantonly and so freakishly imposed." *Id* at 310. Thus the use of capital punishment in America was halted for a short period of time. Immediately, states began to craft revised capital statutes intended to pass constitutional scrutiny under the *Furman* standard.

In four short years, the Court considered several statutes consolidated under *Gregg v. Georgia*, 428 U.S. 153 (1976). In *Gregg*, a 7-2 majority of the Supreme Court upheld as constitutional Georgia's revised capital sentencing scheme, also sustaining similarly revised Florida and Texas schemes, and striking down North Carolina's and Louisiana's attempts to revise their capital statutes. The next term, the Court laid to rest arguments concerning the nature of crimes for which the ultimate sanction was appropriate. Applying a proportionality analysis, the Court held that the imposition of the death penalty for the crime of rape was grossly disproportionate and excessive under the Eighth Amendment. *Coker v. Georgia*, 433 U.S. 584 (1977).

Since *Gregg* brought back the ultimate sanction's utilization, other challenges have been raised against the death penalty which have largely been unsuccessful, though some limited prohibitions have been declared. For example, in *Penry v, Lynaugh* 492 U.S. 302 (1989), the Court ruled that it is not, per se, cruel and unusual punishment to impose the ultimate sanction on a person who is mentally retarded as contrasted with *Ford v. Wainwright* 477 U.S. 399 (1986) decided only three years earlier, holding that insane individuals cannot be executed.

Another example of limited restrictions surrounds age of the perpetrator at the time of the capital crime's commission. In *Stanford v. Kentucky*, 492 U.S. 361 (1989), the Supreme Court found that imposition of death penalty on persons who were 16 or 17 at the time of the crime is not cruel and unusual punishment. In *Thompson v. Oklahoma*, 487 U.S. 815 (1988), however, the Court suggested that imposition of death penalty on a defendant who was 15 at the time of the commission of the offense violates the Eighth and Fourteenth Amendments.

Methods of Execution

While the concept of death as punishment for a crime is well settled as being appropriate under the U.S. Constitution, the method by which the government imposes the ultimate sanction raises a separate issue. With regard to the constitutionality of the methods of execution, the U.S. Supreme Court has never directly addressed this issue.

Most of the cases have dealt with the constitutionality of electrocution as the method of execution. In *In re Kemmler*, 136 U.S. 436 (1890), the Supreme Court was presented with the question of the appropriateness of electrocution as a method of execution provided for by New York statute. As is often the case, the Court chose not to attack the issue directly, but rather relied on the power of the state legislature. The *Kemmler* Court held that the New York law providing for electrocution of the condemned was "within the legitimate sphere of the legislative power of the state." p. 448.

A quarter-century later, the Court was again faced with a similar issue in *Malloy v. South Carolina*, 237 U.S. 180 (1915). In *Malloy*, the Court was asked to assess an amendment to the South Carolina capital punishment statute that changed the method of execution from hanging to electrocution. The Court found that since the statutory amendment did not increase the amount of punishment and since some of the "odious features" of hanging were eliminated by the change to electrocution, the change was found to be constitutionally sound.

The next significant case to address the issue of the method of death, specifically, whether more than one opportunity is given the state in carrying out the condemned person's death, was *Louisiana ex rel. Francis v. Resweber*, 329 U.S. 459 (1946). In *Resweber*, inmate Francis had been prepared for execution and strapped in the chair. The deadly electrical current was released but the chair malfunctioned. Francis was taken back to his cell and a new execution date was set. Francis argued that the trauma of being prepared for execution coupled with his having been strapped in the electric chair and the switch activated but without electrical current running through his body constituted cruel and unusual punishment and should not be allowed a second time. Justice Reed, writing for the Supreme Court, rejected Francis' claim:

> Even the fact that petitioner has already been subjected to a current of electricity does not make his subsequent execution any more cruel in the constitutional sense than any other execution. The cruelty against which the Constitution protects a convicted man is cruelty inherent in the method of punishment, not the necessary suffering involved in any method employed to extinguish life humanely. The fact that an unforeseeable accident prevented the prompt consummation of the sentence cannot, it seems to us, add an element of cruelty to a subsequent execution. There is no purpose to inflict unnecessary pain nor any unnecessary pain involved in the proposed execution. The situation of the unfortunate victim of this accident is just as though he had suffered the identical amount of mental anguish and physical pain in any other occurrence, such as, for example, a fire in the cellblock. We cannot agree that the hardship imposed upon the petitioner rises to that level of hardship denounced as denial of due process because of cruelty (*Resweber*, p. 464).

Thus, the Supreme Court has never directly addressed a method of execution. In 1993, however, one-third of the Supreme Court, in a dissent to a denial of a writ of certiorari, expressed a least a willingness to address the method of execution. See *Poyner v. Murray*, 508 U.S. 931 (1993).

While the U.S. Supreme Court has not addressed the issue of methods of execution directly, some lower federal courts have spoken on the issue. In *Langford v. Day*, 110 F. 3d 1380 (9th Cir.

1997), the court found that execution by hanging did not violate the Eighth Amendment's prohibition against cruel and unusual punishment. In *Fierro v. Gomez*, 77 F. 3d 301 (9th Cir. 1996) (vacated and remanded based on California Penal Code § 3604, see *Gomez v. Fierro*, 519 U.S. 918 (1996)), however, the court found that execution by lethal gas as used by the State of California was cruel and unusual punishment. Finally, in *Wollis v. Mc-Cotter*, 798 F. 2d 695 (5th Cir. 1985), the court found that Wollis' claim that the administration of sodium thiopental in the process of lethal injection of condemned prisoners in Texas did not rise to the level of cruel and unusual punishment under the Eighth Amendment.

Thus, at present, the U.S. Supreme Court has yet to directly confront the constitutionality of a particular method of execution. While some lower federal courts have delved into the intricacies of this issue, those decisions, of course, are only applicable in those particular jurisdictions and offer no real definitive answers. Inevitably, the Supreme Court will have to directly confront the issue of methods of execution. Until that time, such issues will abound in the litigious abyss of the decisional law of the lower federal courts and state courts who may choose to confront the issue directly.

Summary

Capital punishment has existed in one form or the other throughout written history. It has been a controversial disposition for almost as long. The debate appears to have intensified in the Twentieth Century. Both opponents and proponents actively pursue their agendas producing extensive litigation. Most of this litigation has focused on the extent to which capital punishment can be considered cruel and unusual punishment. After a short period of time during which the existing practices were held to fail the cruel and unusual provisions of the Constitution because of the arbitrary nature in which the penalty is imposed, state legislatures in the 38 states choosing to use death as a sanction rewrote their statutes so that the likelihood of the arbitrary application of the death penalty was reduced to the point that constitutional standards were met.

The maintenance of death row inmates creates a number of problems for correctional administrators. Inmates sentenced to death are not committed to the department of corrections in most states. They are county inmates who are held pending the execution of their sentences. In addition, the authorities are charged with preserving the life of the inmate until the death sentence can be carried out. Inmates sentenced to death must also be considered as escape risks. As a result, death row inmates are maintained in segregation units with limited services and an austere environment. The poor quality of life in this environment has been challenged as inappropriate by inmate advocates and death penalty opponents.

Although the death penalty itself has been held to be constitutionally acceptable, the method of execution has been challenged as unnecessarily cruel and unusual. This controversy remains unresolved as various states move from one form of execution to another with each identified as unacceptably painful by death penalty opponents.

This debate is certain to continue to be active well into the Twenty-first Century. Proponents and opponents are struggling to capture public support for their respective positions. This struggle is likely to be expressed in continuing litigation and legislation.

References

Carlson, P.M. (1999) *Prison and jail administration: Practice and theory*. Gaithersburg, MD: Aspen Publishers, Inc.

Deiter, R. (1996). *Twenty years of capital punishment: A reevaluation*. Washington, DC: Death Penalty Information Center.

Hawkins, R., & Alpert, G. P. (1989). *American prison systems: Punishment and justice.* Englewood Cliffs, NJ: Prentice Hall.

Cases

Coker v. Georgia, 433 U.S. 584 (1977)

Fierro v. Gomez, 77 F. 3d 301 (9th Cir. 1996)

Ford v. Wainwright 477 U.S. 399, 106 S.Ct. 2595 (1986)

Gregg v. Georgia, 428 U.S. 153, 96 S.Ct. 2909 (1976)

Furman v. Georgia 408 U.S. 238 (1972)

Harmelin v. Michigan, 501 U.S. 957 (1991)

In Re Kemmler, 136 U. S. 436 (1890)

Langford v. Day, 110 F. 3d 1380 (9th Cir. 1997)

Louisiana ex rel. Francis v. Resweber, 329 U.S. 459 (1946)

Malloy v. South Carolina, 237 U.S. 180 (1915)

McGautha v. California and Crampton v. Ohio [consolidated at 402 U.S. 183] (1971)

Penry v, Lynaugh 492 U.S. 302 (1989)

Poyner v. Murray, 508 U.S. 931 (1993)

Robinson v. California 370 U.S. 660 (1962)

Solem v. Helm, 463 U.S. 277 (1983)

Stanford v. Kentucky, 492 U.S. 361 (1989)

Thompson v. Oklahoma, 487 U.S. 815 (1988)

Wilkerson v. Utah, 99 U. S. 130 (1878)

Wollis v. McCotter, 798 F. 2d 695 (5th Cir. 1985)

Chapter 7

Correctional Privatization and the Constitution

Privatization has been an issue throughout the history of corrections. Privatization has been more common in community corrections than in institutional corrections particularly in the areas of halfway house services and treatment programs. Champion (1990) identifies five issues that continue to be raised in the privatization of the management of correctional facilities: professionalization of administration, public accountability, prison labor, public relations, and political considerations.

Correctional systems turn to privatization to save money. In most systems, the largest single budget items are salaries and benefits. The other items of the budget are generally limited and reflect minimal allocations for the fixed costs needed to complete the tasks and to provide the services mandated by law and judicial decree. Privatization implies that the private agency will make a profit by operating at lower costs. In order to do this, personnel costs must be reduced. While in many cases the new corporate manager retains the existing staff with reduced salaries and benefits, in many cases new relatively inexperienced line officers and managers are hired. Critics suggest that managers and staff who are new to corrections lack sufficient skills and knowledge (professionalization) to effectively operate the facility (Cohn, 1987).

Public accountability has generated legal controversy. Only public entities have the legal authority to sanction. The constitutional legitimacy of privatization of management will be reviewed in depth in the following pages as will the issue of prison labor.

While the public has been reluctant to endorse the privatization of prisons (Bowditch & Everett, 1987; Logan, 1987), some studies indicate that the public may be more accepting of the concept (Jengeleski, 1986; Cullen, 1986). The public has mixed feeling about who is best suited to manage prisons. On the one hand, the public believes that the profit motive can lead to efficient and effective operations. On the other, the public suspects that cutting costs can lead to the use of unethical approaches to treatment and a reduced quality in operations. Political considerations tend to be similar to public considerations with the added element of loss of control of the system and its budget by political leaders (Bowditch & Everett, 1987; Durham, 1987; Pellicciotti, 1987).

Institutional privatization issues related to litigation can be loosely categorized into three categories: the provision of specific services under contract, the use of inmate labor to produce consumable goods, and the management of correctional programs and facilities. Of these, the use of prison labor tends to be historical while medical and management services have generated contemporary litigation .

The types of services which have been provided through contract with the private sector has been very broad including such things as food service and laundry but also very limited with two exceptions. Some correctional systems and specific institutions have contracted with private service providers for specific treatment programs. These programs can be relatively broad, as in the case of the use of therapeutic communities to reduce recidivism, or very narrow, as in the case of treatment programs for sexual offenders. The most common service contracted privately is medical services. Privatization of medical services range from contracts with local service providers such as doctors, nursing homes, and hospitals with inmates transported to the private facility or office for services to complete medical services for the system delivered within the institutions by an independent service provider. In the latter case, the provider hires staff, provides supplies, and sets policy while institutional staff provide supervision of the inmates and maintain security. Private provision of contract services has not been legally controversial. In many cases, private contracting has been a response to legal challenges regarding the quality of services provided by the institution.

Historical Issues

The use of prison labor by private industry has the longest and most controversial history as a point of contention that has produced legal challenges. The use of prison labor to produce goods which are then sold on the open market actually predates the development of the modern prison system (Bates, 1937). Early English jails used inmates to produce products such as oakum used to caulk the seams in the wooden sailing ships of the day. In the United States, early prison systems both operated prison industries which produced products for the market and convict lease systems in which private corporations used cheap prison labor to produce goods for the open market. Both labor and business owners opposed the use of prison labor to produce goods for the open market because those businesses that had access to inmates had a competitive advantage (competition with labor for jobs and with competitors in reduced costs). This issue became salient in the 1930s and a number of federal legislative initiatives reduced the freedom of the Federal Bureau of Prisons to use prison labor. The Hawes-Cooper Act, the Federal Prison Labor Law, and The National Recovery Act all sought to prevent prison labor from being utilized, since such use would probably have meant the unemployment of some free citizen (Bates, 1937). The business and labor coalition continued to work together to oppose the use of prison labor to compete in the open market and all states presently have state use statutes. These statutes specify that products produced by prison labor can only be used in public facilities with specific exceptions in some states for farm products.

Between the late 1930s and the early 1970s, the corrections industries programs in the United States and Canada slipped into a neglected niche; however, the middle to late 1970s saw a renewed interest on the parts of both areas of corrections in the possible rehabilitative benefits that could be gained through the use of such programs. Gandy and Hurl (1987) explained this phenomenon as an acknowledgement of the ability to improve chances of rehabilitation, reduce chances that inmates would recidivate, and increase the stability of the population.

Contemporary Initiatives

Recent innovations such as work release have been authorized under statutes that specify that inmates who work in private sector jobs must be paid the prevailing wage for the type of work that they perform. A limited number of cooperative projects have been implemented in which a business establishes a production facility within or adjacent to the correctional facility. The statutes authorizing these operations also specify that working inmates be paid prevailing wages. As a result of the careful approach which correctional program developers have taken to avoid unfair competition in creating these programs and in gaining the support of labor, there are no contemporary legal challenges to their operation.

The third category, management of correctional facilities, has generated considerable contemporary controversy. Arguments surrounding the rehabilitative impact of prisons draw sharp debate from both sides of the issue, and the case is the same with the issue of privatizing our nation's prisons and jails. Privatization of prisons flowed from the need of the Federal Bureau of Prisons and the many state and territorial departments of correction to get the maximum value for each dollar budgeted for prison operation and administration. The popular political response to the demand to "get tough on crime" necessarily meant increasing the number of beds available to incarcerate convicted criminals. As

Savas (1987) asserts, the privatization of prisons attempts to meet the public outcry for more incarceration for less, as evidenced by the electorate's unwillingness to finance more beds, while attempting to turn a profit in the process.

The increasing numbers of beds coupled with a reluctance to increase taxes created pressure for the streamlining of correctional budgets. Our nation's embracing of the free market ideal caused governments to look to the private sector to address these needs. This had led to the increased use of prison privatization over the last decade.

There are four models for privatization of management: the contractor operates a facility owned by the political unit responsible for the inmates; the political unit constructs a new facility for management by a private contractor (funding through public bonds); the contractor builds and operates a facility under contract with a specific political unit; and the private contractor builds a facility and accepts inmates from multiple political units on a cost per bed basis. While the contractual issues and management approaches differ considerably, contemporary legal challenges are similar regardless of the approach taken.

The privatization of management in American corrections began to gain attention and take hold in the mid 1980s. Robbins (1987) identified four key advantages and three major hurdles in the privatization of corrections. One advantage lay in the fact that the government had done a questionable job in prison management. Soaring costs, failure in rehabilitating inmates, and inhuman conditions in the prisons have been advanced as evidence of a real need to change course. A second advantage lies in anticipated reduced costs. As a general rule, the private sector can provide the same service as government but at a much cheaper cost, in some cases as much as 40% savings. (Savas, 1987). Third, prison overcrowding might be alleviated by privatization. As Savas (1987) points out, the private sector is quicker and more flexible when it comes to prison construction. For example, where government would have to get electoral approval of a bond issue to finance a new institution, the private company needs no voter approval. The private company uses private capital to build the prison and recoups its investment when the government makes annual payments to the company to house its inmates. The fourth advantage identified by Robbins is the belief that privatization will reduce legal liability. It was believed that if the government privatized its prisons, state legal liability would decrease as the contractor would assume much of the liability now encumbered on the state. Gold (1996) also recognizes two advantages to privatizing our correctional institutions. First, private firms are better able to provide modern physical facilities for any security level. Second, the cost of correctional services, such as medical care and food, are cheaper because there are more choices available on the open market to private contractors.

The three major hurdles to privatization of prisons include the fact that government cannot contract away its § 1983 liability for prisoners' rights abuses, a serious concern as to the appropriateness of government delegating broad authority to the private sector, and the problem of profit-motive by the private contractors (Robbins, 1987). Other long term problems may arise as well, such as labor disputes by the private sector employees which raises the question of who would operate the institution in the event of a strike or in the event of bankruptcy by a prison management company. As Robbins (1987) notes prison operation is not a short-term business. As such, we must carefully approach and plan private management of prisons with an eye to the future.

From the public policy front, Farris (1998) has identified four major concerns with the privatization of corrections: a total lack of financial disinterestedness by private contractors in the operation of correctional facilities, a lack of real cost savings when considering the costs of monitoring the contract and the state's loss of sovereign immunity over its prison operations, less protection of prisoners' fundamental rights, and the concession that the government cannot efficiently and effectively manage its prisons. Ratliff (1997) maintains that while the present prison privatization movement has serious constitutional due process shortcomings, privately operated institutions can provide significant cost-savings and better quality services if carefully monitored by the controlling governmental authority. Without close oversight, however, governments' privatization experiments will be an abysmal failure. As Silvester (1990) correctly points out, the privatization of prisons is markedly different from privatization in the traditional commercial setting, specifically in free choice. For example, in the entertainment industry, if the service one receives is inadequate and substandard, patrons will not support the business and can choose another provider or another form of entertainment. Ultimately, the business will fail. Not so with prisons, as the patrons, the inmates, are not there by their free choice but are there under government order.

Ratliff (1997) notes that in order to insure success, the profit motive and absolute lack of financial disinterestedness of private firms operating prisons must be recognized and dealt with appropriately, especially where privatization contracts provide for per diem reimbursement based on the number of inmates housed. To address the problem of financial bias regarding per diem reimbursement, Ratliff (1997) suggests that the government authority should retain control over classification, release, and discipline decisions.

42 U.S.C. § 1983 and Privatization of Prisons

As outlined above, there are several possible problems with privatizing our nation's prisons. Arguably, the one greatest problem that has emerged is the protection of prisoners' rights in privately operated institutions of correction. The State of Tennessee has, in many respects, been the role model for the privatization movement as it was one of the first states to experiment in contracting total management of its correctional facilities to the private sector. It is in a Tennessee case that the U.S. Supreme Court decided a recent § 1983 claim where the issue was whether private prison guards were afforded qualified immunity from § 1983 liability as state actors. Prior to this decision, judicial decisions had been mixed with regard to granting employees of private correctional management companies immunity from § 1983 liability (*Citrano v. Allen Correctional Center*, 891 F. Supp. 312 (W.D. La. 1995); *Manis v. Corrections Corporation of America*, 859 F. Supp. 302 (M.D. Tenn. 1994)).

In *Richardson v. McKnight* (1997), however, the United States Supreme Court ruled that prisons guards employed by private prison management firms who are under contract with the state do not enjoy the protections of immunity from suit under 42 U.S.C. § 1983 as state actors. The decision caused ripples throughout the privatization movement and caused providers of private correctional services to more closely assess their liability in this regard.

Ronnie McKnight, an inmate at the South Tennessee Correctional Center in Clifton, Tennessee, sought tort damages from Richardson, a guard at the facility and his colleague, John Walker. McKnight alleged that the officers, during a transport, placed restraints on his legs too tightly and injured him then demonstrated a deliberate indifference to his serious medical needs. The U.S. District Court and the Sixth Circuit Court of Appeals sided with McKnight, noting that Tennessee had privatized its corrections' program and that the correctional officers were employees of the contracting company and not the state. The U.S. Supreme Court, in a close 5-4 decision written by Justice Breyer, affirmed the court of appeals.

Justice Breyer, relying on *Wyatt v. Cole* (1992), reiterated that the purpose of § 1983 was to prevent state actors from, under their authority, disregarding one's federally guaranteed rights. Section 1983, according to Breyer, can sometimes impose liability on a private individual when that private individual is acting for the state. While *Wyatt* did not answer the specific question presented in *McKnight*, it did provide that in order to find the answer the Court had to look to history and to the traditional and special policy concerns associated with suing government officials.

In looking to the historical application of § 1983, Breyer found no patterned application of the civil rights provision in the context of private prison guards. Breyer also noted the competitive economic nature of the private prison industry. Private correctional management firms seek to profit from assuming the states' responsibilities in operating prisons, and there is little direct state supervision. While the guards in this instance were not held to enjoy immunity, Breyer did limit the scope of *McKnight*: the only issue this case resolved was the question of immunity under § 1983. It did not decide if Richardson and his colleague were liable under the section despite the fact they are employed by private firm; the immunity question here was decided on its facts, where a private firm assumes a major state administrative task with little or no direct state supervision; and, this case makes no comment on whether or not the defendants could raise a good faith defense, outside pure immunity under § 1983

Justice Scalia dissented, arguing that the majority misapplied § 1983 by relying on the status of the defendants and not on the function they performed. If one looks at the function performed, prison management, such is clearly a state action. Analogizing to special prosecutors appointed in local jurisdictions to conduct highly charged criminal actions, Scalia thinks that such specially appointed, *private* prosecutors would be immune. Likewise, in Scalia's view, private prison managers/guards should enjoy the same treatment. Scalia fears that this decision will contribute, unnecessarily, to the costs of correctional privatization.

The *McKnight* decision has been relied on by several courts to deny § 1983 immunity to private sector prison employees and has been used to expand into other collateral areas. In *Lemoine v. New Horizons Ranch and Center, Inc.* (1998), a U.S. district court in Texas held that a juvenile treatment facility and its employees were subject to § 1983 liability as state actors. The center involved was a residential treatment facility for problem youth located in a very rugged environment. A young man was committed there and placed on medication that made him less tolerant to extreme heat. After a rules violation, the resident juvenile was assigned to build a rock wall in the sweltering heat. The juvenile collapsed and died of what was later determined to be a stroke. The mother, suing on behalf of her deceased son's estate, alleged that the center and its employees, especially the medical

personnel, were liable under § 1983, as state actors, for proscribing her son medication known to make one extra-sensitive to
heat. The district court agreed with the mother, analogizing to
the private prison situation in *McKnight*. Similarly, the Ninth
Circuit Court of Appeals has applied the *McKnight* standard to a
detoxification facility under contract with government entities
to provide such services. The facility argued that since they were
a not-for-profit corporation, the concerns raised by the profit
motive in privatization did not apply to them. The Court dismissed that argument noting that both profit and not-for-profit
facilities compete for government contacts (*Halvorsen, Jr. v.
Baird*, 1998).

Courts in Alabama and Florida have also applied *McKnight* to
deny immunity to privately employed correctional personnel.
(*McDuffie v. Hopper*, 1997; *Nelson v. Prison Health Services, Inc.*,
1997). It should be noted, however, at least one court has recognized the open question in *McKnight* as to whether private personnel, in this case a doctor, can claim the good faith defense
available to public employees under § 1983 (*Robinson v. City of
San Bernardino, et al.*, 1998). Thus, more litigation on this question can be expected.

Summary

Privatization of correctional services is an old issue. The use of
inmate labor to produce products for the open market has been
present for as long as society has detained other men and women
because of their misdeeds. The inmate labor issue was effectively
resolved in the 1930s and contemporary programs such as work
release and cooperative programs between correctional staff and
private citizens create work places in or near prisons have been
carefully developed to assure both labor and management that inmate labor will not create an unfair competitive advantage in the
market place. The use of private contracts to provide specific services tends to be a response to litigation rather than a cause of lit-

igation. Much of the controversy has centered on the provision of adequate medical care, which is addressed in Chapter 8.

The privatization of management of correctional facilities has created controversy for a number of reasons. The most litigated issue has been the application of § 1983 to private corrections. The courts have indicated that § 1983 claims can be brought against private persons who assume state responsibility for sentenced offenders. In essence, liability for constitutional violations cannot be escaped by the states by contracting the management of correctional facilities to private entities. The issue of the application of acceptable defenses granted state employees, such as the good faith rule, for private corrections staff has not been decided and is likely to be the subject of future litigation.

We can also anticipate litigation from a new initiative. Private correctional facilities have begun to build prisons to hold inmates from jurisdictions from correctional systems and courts outside of the geographical area in which the prison is located. Public resistance is building from both the residents living in the area in which the prison is built and from families of the inmates who are transferred away from home. At some point, these groups are likely to express their dissatisfaction in litigation.

References

Bates, S. (1937). *Prisons and beyond.* New York: MacMillan.

Bowditch, C., & Everett, R.S. (1987). Private prisons: Problems within the solution. *Justice Quarterly, 4,* 441-453.

Champion, D.J. (1990). *Corrections in the United States.* Englewood Cliffs, NJ: Prentice Hall.

Cohn, A.W. (1987). The failure of correctional management: The potential for reversal. *Federal Probation, 51,* 3-7

Cullen, F.T. (1986). The privatization of treatment: Prison reform in the 1980s. *Federal Probation, 50,* 8-16.

Durham, A.M., III (1987). Correctional privatization and the justice model: The collision of justice and utility. *Journal of Comtemporaty Criminal Justice, 3*, 57-69.

Farris, L.S. (1998). Private jails in Oklahoma: An unconstitutional delegation of legislative authority. *Tulsa Law Journal, 33,* 959-977.

Gandy, J. & Hurl, L. (1987). Private sector involvement in prison industries: Options and issues. *London Journal of Criminology, 229*(2), 185-204.

Gold, M.E. (1996). The privatization of prisons. *The Urban Lawyer, 28,* 359-389.

Jengeleski, J.I., (1986). Corrections a move to privatization. In B. I. Wolford and P. Lawrenz, (Eds). *Issues in correctional training and casework.* College Park, MD: American Correctional Association.

Logan, C.H. (1987). The propriety of proprietary prisons. *Federal Probation, 51,* 35-40.

Pelliccotti, J.M. (1987). 42 U.S.C. Sec. 1983 & correctional officials liability: A look to the new century. *Journal of Contemporary Criminal Justice, 3,* 1-9.

Ratliff, W.L. (1997). The due process failure of America's prison privatization statutes. *Seton Hall Legislative Journal, 21,* 371-424.

Robbins, I.P. (1987). Privatization of corrections: Defining the issues. *Vanderbilt Law Review, 40,* 813-828.

Savas, E.S. (1987). Privatization and prisons. *Vanderbilt Law Review, 40,* 889-899.

Silvester, D.B. (1990). Ethics and privatization in criminal justice: Does education have a role to play? *Journal of Criminal Justice, 18,* 65-70.

Cases

Citrano v. Allen Correctional Center, 891 F. Supp. 312 (W.D. La. 1995)

Halvorsen, Jr. v. Baird, 146 F. 3d 680 (9th Cir. 1998)

Lemoine v. New Horizons Ranch and Center, Inc., et al., 990 F. Supp. 498 (N.D. Tex. 1998)

Manis v. Corrections Corporation of America, 859 F. Supp. 302 (M.D. Tenn. 1994)

McDuffie v. Hopper, 982 F. Supp. 817 (M.D. Ala. 1997)

Nelson v. Prison Health Services, Inc., 991 F. Supp. 1452 (M.D. Fla. 1997).

Richardson v. McKnight, 521 U.S. 399 (1997)

Robinson v. City of San Bernardino, et al., 992 F. Supp. 1198 (C.D. Cal. 1998)

Smith v. United States, 850 F. Supp. 984 (M.D. Fla. 1994)

Tinnen v. Corrections Corporation of America, 1993 WL 738121 (W.D. Tenn. 1993)

Wyatt v. Cole, 504 U.S. 158 (1992)

Chapter 8

Institutional Medical Care

No issue has been as central to the development of inmate rights as the provision of medical treatment. Deprivation of medical care provides sensational cases due to the degree and nature of the damage caused by failure to provide effective and timely medical care. Medical care was a central issue in the cases that breached the hands-off doctrine and provided the basis for the articulation of the deliberate indifference principle, which emerged as litigation shaped the manner in which correctional managers operate their institutions.

While not central, medical care was an element in the complaint and response in the challenge to the constitutionality of the Arkansas system. The issue of medical care was more central in the case of litigation brought against the Department of Corrections in Alabama. The first complaint brought against the State of Alabama alleged that inmates held in Alabama prisons were denied effective medical care and that this denial violated the cruel and unusual provisions of the Eighth Amendment. In 1972, the federal court held that the level of basic medical care in Alabama institutions for prisoners was inadequate to the point that inmates were exposed to conditions which constituted a violation of the cruel and unusual provisions of the Eighth Amendment (*Newman v. Alabama*, 1972). This decision was followed in 1976 by litigation asserting that the operation of the prison system in its totality was a violation of the Eighth Amendment (*Pugh v. Locke*, 1976). The court found for the plaintiffs and ordered comprehensive reform in the operation of institutions managed by the Alabama Department of Corrections including minimum standards for medical care.

The issue of adequate medical care is complicated by the absence of clear standards for medical care in the broader community and by the wide variety in mechanisms for the delivery of medical services in correctional environments. Debates regarding availability of insurance or subsidized medical care to all citizens, the quality of services delivered by health management organizations, the standards for the denial of specific procedures by some medical plans, and the debate as to the level of care due the poor influenced and still influence the perspectives held by citizens and correctional managers. Historically, medical services in corrections were provided through use of a wide range of mechanisms including taking inmates to community health care providers, visiting physicians, nurses and physicians' assistants, and 'trained' inmates. Some of the latter were trained professionals who were incarcerated; others learned their skills in the prison infirmary. Setting clear and consistent standards for medical care, given the contentiousness of the health care debate in society at large and the wide range of delivery structures, was beyond the courts and might explain the preference for assessing intent of the administrators and medical personnel inherent in the deliberate indifference standard.

Leading Cases

Medical care was first addressed within broad sweeping decisions. In *Jackson v. Bishop* (1968) and *Holt v. Sarver* (1969), basic living conditions and the operation of the Arkansas Prison System in and of itself, including the provision of medical care, was held to be in violation of the cruel and unusual punishment provisions of the Eighth Amendment. In 1972, the issue was approached directly when the federal court ruled on medical care in *Newman v. Alabama* (1972). The court found for the plaintiffs and ordered comprehensive reform in the operation of institutions managed by the Alabama Department of Corrections including the provision of adequate medical care.

The leading case in this area is *Estelle v. Gamble* (1976). In *Estelle*, the U.S. Supreme Court held that the entity that is holding the inmate is responsible for providing medical care. Unnecessary delay in providing necessary medical treatment is a violation of the Cruel and Unusual Punishment Clause of the Eighth Amendment. The Court set forth a standard of deliberate indifference by which institutional medical care will be judged. In effect, this standard places on the inmate the burden to show that the institutional officials demonstrated a deliberate indifference to a serious medical need by not providing proper treatment. Absent a showing of deliberate indifference on the part of institutional officials, the inmate has no claim.

In *Estelle*, inmate J.W. Gamble suffered a back strain while unloading a bale of cotton from a truck. For approximately one month after the injury, he was treated by prison medical personnel with medication and allowed to stay in his cell. After a month, the attending physician, despite Gamble's claims that he was still in pain, continued the medication, but cleared him for some work. Gamble continued to complain of back pain and was placed in administrative segregation. Gamble appeared before the institutional disciplinary authority for his refusal to work. When the committee learned of his back injury and his alleged high blood pressure, they ordered that he been seen by another physician.

The next day, Gamble was examined by another physician who prescribed medication for the high blood pressure and continued the pain relievers. The next week, Gamble saw the doctor again who continued the blood pressure medication for an additional month. Twice more Gamble visited the prison hospital where additional medication for his back pain was prescribed. During this period, Gamble remained in administrative segregation. After approximately another month, Gamble was again cleared for light work but refused citing now his back injury and severe headaches. He again saw a physician who prescribed another pain medication and continued his blood pressure medication. Gamble again appeared before the prison disciplinary committee for his refusal to work. Gamble cited his back injury and his blood pressure condition for his inability to work; however, a medical assistant testified that Gamble's medical condition should not keep him from working. Based on this testimony, Gamble was placed in solitary confinement.

Four mornings later, Gamble complained of chest discomfort and having "blank outs" (*Estelle v. Gamble*,1976 at 101). Some 12 hours later, he was examined by a medical assistant and hospitalized. The next day, he was examined by a doctor who performed a heart rhythm test and was placed on medication for an irregular heartbeat and moved to administrative segregation. The next day, Gamble complained of chest and left arm pain as well as back pain and requested to see a physician. His request was denied for two days. Finally, Gamble was allowed to see the doctor who continued the heart medicine for another three days. During this period, Gamble filed his complaint that eventually made its way to the U.S. Supreme Court.

The Court evaluated this issue on Eighth Amendment grounds. Prior decisions of the Court had laid the groundwork for Eighth Amendment analysis. In this case, the Court found that the government is obligated to provide medical care for the incarcerated because those persons have no other access to medical care. If the government does not provide this medical care, unnecessary suffering and even death may result.

The Court, per Justice Marshall, established a "deliberate indifference" standard that would apply in determining if inmates received adequate medical care (*Estelle v. Gamble*, 1976 at 104). This indifference may be on the part of a prison doctor's treatment (or refusal to treat) or a correctional officer's refusal to seek care or interference with a prescribed treatment after the fact. In all cases, however, the actions of institutional officials in interfering or denying treatment must be intentional. For example, mere medical malpractice would not rise to the level of a constitutional violation. Rather, the acts or omissions must demonstrate deliberative inaction on the part of prison officials to a prisoner's medical need. Mere negligence, alone, will not give rise to a cause of action under this standard.

In Gamble's case, the deliberate indifference standard was not proved by the petitioner. During the three month period preceding Gamble's suit, he was examined by medical personnel on 17 different occasions. This can hardly be said to demonstrate a deliberate, intentional denial or interference by prison officials of medical treatment to the inmate.

Recent Cases

Recently, several courts have applied the *Estelle* standard to both grant and deny inmate relief. The Seventh Circuit Court of Appeals ruled against an inmate who raised an *Estelle* claim because she contracted tuberculosis while she was incarcerated. The petitioner-inmate claimed that correctional officials were deliberately indifferent to her serious medical needs by allowing TB to be spread through the prison and that the treatment she received post-diagnosis was insufficient (*Forbes v. Edgar*, 7th Cir. 1997). The court rejected both claims. First, there was no credible evidence that prison authorities deliberately allowed the infection to be spread throughout the prison, despite the inmate's claim that one inmate with active TB remained out of isolation and with the general population. Thorough screening procedures were in place to guard against the disease reaching the entire population. Thus, the *Estelle* standard was met in this case. In another case, the Fifth Circuit ruled against an inmate who had persistent problems with rectal prolapse and claimed prison officials were deliberately indifferent to his serious medical needs. Over a two-year period, the inmate had repeated difficulty with retracting rectal muscles after a bowel movement and required physical reinsertion of rectal tissue. Prison medical staff assisted the inmate on many occasions with this need and additionally provided him with medical supplies that would allow him to complete the task himself. Unfortunately, the problem did not respond to treatment and the inmate filed an *Estelle* challenge alleging that the prison was deliberately indifferent to his serious medical need (*Norton v. Dimazana*, 5th Cir. 1997). Despite the inmate's unfortunate situation, he failed to show that the prison personnel violated the *Estelle* standard. The inmate's institutional medical records were illustrative of the extensive treatment and assistance he received for his condition. Over the period in question, he was examined by doctors, generalists and specialists, at least once a month both on-grounds and off-grounds, he was granted recovery time in his cell, and his work status was changed because of his medical condition. Thus, again, the deliberate indifference standard was not satisfied. Lastly, the Second Circuit Court of Appeals has applied the standard to provide an inmate with relief. In *Koehl v. Dalsheim* (1996), the inmate alleged that his prescription eyeglasses were necessary to prevent him from experiencing double vision and flawed depth perception. The court found that while these conditions do not cause suffering, they are sufficient to be out of line with the contemporary standards of decency recognized in *Estelle*. Contra, an inmate who lost his eyesight after release from prison sued claiming that the prison doctors should have discovered a tumor that ultimately resulted in his blindness. Medical records showed that doctors examined the inmate on several occasions and fit him with glasses. The tumor, however, was not discovered by prison doctors. Thus, the federal appellate court found that, absent a showing by the inmate that the doctors knew about the tumor and deliberately ignored it and failed to treat it, the *Estelle* standard was not offended. (*Johnson v. Quinones*, et al., 1998).

Three other cases are illustrative of how state courts have applied the *Estelle* standard in state proceedings. First, in *Mourning v. Correctional Medical Services* (N.J. Super. App. Div. 1997), the court rejected an inmate's challenge to a state requirement of co-payment of medical expenses. The inmate claimed that the co-payment scheme constituted cruel and unusual punishment. But, the New Jersey court rejected this argument, noting that while the state must provide medical care for those it incarcerates, there is no rule of law saying that the state must also bear the entire economic burden associated with prison medical care (*Mourning* at 539). Further, the New Jersey statutes provide that treatment will not be withheld based on an inmate's inability to pay. Next, an Alabama appellate court, in *Perry v. Department of Corrections* (Ala. Civ. App. 1997), dismissed an inmate's claim of deliberate indifference to a serious medical need in the denial of reconstructive surgery. Prior to his imprisonment, the inmate had a colostomy. The inmate petitioned the institutional authorities for the requested surgery so that he would "be able to dispose [of] body wastes like a normal human being." In this case, however, institutional medical personnel concluded that the reconstructive surgery was not a medical necessity and there was evidence to show that prison officials supplied the inmate with colostomy bags and his condition was monitored on a regular basis by medical personnel. Finally, the Oregon Court of Appeals has rejected claims of an excessively obese inmate that his obesity was a medical need that was treated indifferently by prison authorities. In *Shelton v. Armenakis*, the inmate, who weighed approximately 500 pounds, was in danger of losing his legs because of his condition and was told he must reduce his weight to avoid this loss. The inmate claimed that he should have been placed on a diet to assist him in reducing his weight; however, the court rejected this notion, holding that disagreement on how to treat a condition does not satisfy the deliberate indifference standard required by law.

Another issue in prison medicine that has arisen is whether an inmate may be forcibly medicated against his will. In the mental health context, the U.S. Supreme Court has found that such treatment is constitutionally sound so long as the treatment is shown to be medically necessary and is undertaken to protect the prisoner from himself and to prevent harm to others. In *Washington v. Harper* (1990), the Court sustained a policy of the State of Washington providing for forced medication of mentally ill prisoners. While recognizing the important liberty interests of the prisoner to refuse treatment, Justice Kennedy, writing for the

Court, asserted that the Due Process Clause permits forced medication "if the inmate is dangerous to himself or others and the treatment is in the inmate's medical interest" (*Washington v. Harper,* 1990 at 227).

The Court, however, made clear that forced medication is allowable as long as procedural safeguards are in place. Despite the petitioner's argument that a court must be involved in such an invasion into an inmate's liberty interest, Justice Kennedy found that "the Constitution does not prohibit the State from permitting medical personnel to make the decision under fair procedural mechanisms" (*Washington v. Harper,* 1990 at 231). Thus, a court need not approve of such forcible treatment as long as the institution has in place adequate due process protections.

In *McCormick v. Stadler* (1997), the Fifth Circuit Court of Appeals considered whether an inmate's forced therapy for tuberculosis was appropriate. In *McCormick,* the court found that such forced treatment was constitutional because of the compelling need of the institution to prevent the spread of tuberculosis. The prison's policy "is a rational means of discharging the prison's duty" to protect others from exposure to this disease (*McCormick v. Stadler,* 1997 at 1061). Further, "even if McCormick had some substantive due process right not to be forcibly medicated...for his own benefit as well as that of the prison—the prison's policy..." would be constitutionally sound (*McCormick v. Stadler,* 1997 at 1062). The Eighth Circuit Court of Appeals, however, in *Doby v. Hickerson* (1997) sustained an award of damages to a former Arkansas inmate who had been forcibly medicated with antipsychotic medication. In this case, the proscribing physician did not comply with the procedural safeguards in place in the prison for forced medical treatment before administering the medication. The inmate suffered severe side effects from the medication including Parkinson's-type symptoms. The trial court's award of $9,500 in compensatory damages was sustained.

Another area that has recently been addressed regarding inmate health has been inmate exposure to environmental tobacco smoke (ETS). In *Helling v. McKinney* (1993), the inmate, a nonsmoker, asserted that he was subjected to cruel and unusual punishment because he was celled with a chain smoking inmate and that the exposure to his cellmate's tobacco smoke was harmful to his health. The defendants argued that absent a showing of then current medical problems arising from the exposure to the tobacco smoke, the inmate had no claim.

The Supreme Court rejected the defendants' position. The Court, per Justice White, held that the Eighth Amendment protects prisoners from future harm that may arise from their confinement. "It would be odd to deny [relief] to inmates who plainly proved an unsafe, life-threatening condition in their prison on the ground that nothing yet had happened to them" *Helling v. McKinney,* 1993 at 33). In order to succeed on such a claim, however, an inmate must prove that exposure to ETS is against contemporary standards of human decency and that institutional officials have been deliberately indifferent under *Estelle* to the condition. "The prisoner must show that the risk of which he complains is not one that today's society chooses to tolerate" (*Helling v. McKinney,* 1993 at 36).

In a recent decision, the Eighth Circuit Court of Appeals considered a claim of an inmate's exposure to ETS. In that case, the inmate's claim was denied because he failed to establish the deliberate indifference necessary for a valid claim. Institutional records showed that the inmate was moved to a smoke-free cell, that misconduct reports were issued against inmate's cellmate for smoking, and that the cell was searched for tobacco products. Additionally, the inmate was instructed to contact institutional officials if further problems arose, which the inmate never did. Therefore, the inmate did not meet the *Estelle* test (*Weaver v. Clarke,* 1997 at 854).

Systemic Impact

Eighth Amendment decisions regarding medical services appear to be the decisions which have had both the greatest impact and the most positive results of those decisions which have attempted to address correctional reform though promotion of inmate rights. In most cases, departments of corrections turned to medical professionals when they developed programs to respond to the court's decisions regarding the degree of medical care due to an incarcerated inmate. While the systems which emerged from these widely dispersed efforts varied considerably in form and structure, most appear to deliver quality medical care to inmates with little abuse and little negative consequences other than the added expense. The cost of quality medical care is high regardless of the environment in which the care is delivered.

Privatization of medical services grew rapidly following the *Estelle* decision. Some departments enter into contracts with private medical providers to provide medical services throughout the system. Other departments contract for medical services for specific institutions. In these contractual situations, the department of corrections does not deliver medical services. The medical unit works in the physical setting provided by the department of corrections but provides medical services independent of the department. They recruit and train all medical staff, make all medical decisions, and deliver all medical treatment. In some cases, all services are delivered within the confines of the institution; in some cases, more intensive medical services are provided in community facilities. These operations are medical programs and follow current medical protocols, practices, and policies.

There has also been an increase in comprehensive health care facilities within the institution. New prisons, which are designed to hold inmates who need to be held in a secure environment, include the equivalent of a small hospital within the security perimeter. These facilities include operating theaters and are capable of supporting all but the most sophisticated of surgical procedures. There has also been an increase in the use of centralized medical facilities. That is, one or more institutions will offer extensive medical services. Inmates who require extensive medical care are transferred to these facilities.

What does appear to be common to all of these models is that the delivery of services is designed and maintained by qualified medical personal who have substantial independence in the delivery of their services. This factor assures that medical services meet minimal standards and reduces the exposure of departments of corrections to successful litigation by inmate advocates based on quality of medical care.

Summary

It is clear that courts are willing to entertain inmate claims regarding their medical care. As with all legal claims, mere allegations are insufficient to support a valid claim. In order to prove medical inadequacies in an institutional sitting, an inmate must show that his particular medical need was serious in nature and that contemporary standards of decency would not tolerate the non-treatment of that condition. Further, the inmate must meet the deliberate indifference standard of *Estelle*, demonstrating that the institutional official(s) were more than merely negligence in their response to the condition. Inmates do not need to show that the inaction on the part of the officials was undertaken to specifically harm the inmate.

Given the nature of the response which departments of corrections have made to *Estelle*, it is probable that medical issues will not dominate litigation in the near future. Such litigation as does occur will likely address the boundaries of minimal acceptable care and may mirror the public controversy regarding coverage of the costs associated with elective surgery and experimental treatments from insurance carriers. That is the issue will be whether a particular intervention is necessary for minimal health maintenance.

Cases

Doby v. Hickerson, 120 F. 3d 111 (8th Cir. 1997)

Estelle v. Gamble, 429 U.S. 97 (1976)

Forbes v. Edgar, 112 F. 3d 262 (7th Cir. 1997)

Helling v. McKinney, 509 U.S. 25 (1993)

Holt v. Sarver, 300 F. Supp. 825 (M.D. Ark. 1969)

Johnson v. Quinones, et al., 145 F. 3d 164 (4th Cir. 1998)

Koehl v. Dalsheim, 85 F. 3d 86 (2d Cir. 1996)

McCormick v. Stadler, 105 F. 3d 1059 (5th Cir. 1997)

Mourning v. Correctional Medical Services, 692 A. 2d 213 (N.J. Super. App. 1997)

Newman v. Alabama, 349 F. Supp. 278 (M.D. Ala. 1972)

Norton v. Dimazana, 122 F. 3d 286 (5th Cir. 1997)

Perry v. Department of Corrections, 694 So. 2d 24 (Ala. Civ. App. 1997)

Pugh v. Locke, 406 F. Supp. 318 (M.D. Ala. 1976)

Shelton v. Armenakis, 934 P. 2d 512 (Or. App. 1997)

Washington v. Harper, 419 U.S. 210 (1990)

Weaver v. Clark, 120 F. 3d 852 (8th Cir. 1997)

Chapter 9

Discipline and Inmate Control

Inmate discipline and control cover broad areas. Control in particular has been involved in a broad range of issues. Control addresses the extent to which inmates must obey the rules and regulations of the institution and the orders of the officers while discipline address the extent and nature of the penalties assessed and the process through which guilt and penalties are determined. As a result, many of the more focused complaints such as free expression of religious beliefs and freedom of speech contain substantial control issues: the extent to which correctional representatives can control these activities. Many of the early cases that addressed fundamental living conditions focused on the living conditions in disciplinary units as cruel and unusual punishment with a collateral interest in other basic constitutional rights. This chapter will focus on issues raised regarding the disciplinary process, search procedures, and seizure procedures including restrictions on communications such as magazines, visits, telephone access, and visits.

Control of the inmate population in the correctional institution has several dimensions: control of inmate movement within the institution, control of material which the inmate can have in his or her possession, control of access to the outside world (communications, reading material, basic resources, and visits), and control of the type and timing of activities in which the inmate can participate. To maintain this control, the institution promulgates a series of regulations regarding inmate conduct. When an inmate violates these regulations he or she enters the disciplinary process which includes a finding of fact process, a disposition process with an appeal process, and a satisfaction of the disposition process (loss of good time, reduction in custody grade, reassignment of housing or work, transfer to punitive segregation).

The functional purpose of this control is to prevent escapes and riots, to protect the safety of visitors and employees, to protect state property from damage, protect the safety of inmates, and to protect inmate property from damage. Correctional institutions are managed by relatively small numbers of correctional officers. The security staff inmate ratio is commonly as low as 1 or 2 to 300 on some shifts. In order to enable small numbers of staff to control large numbers of inmates, uniformity of possessions and activities is mandated in most institutions with the amount of freedom of individual inmate expression declining as the security level of the institution and the custody grade of the inmates increases. In secure institutions, a wide range of activities are prohibited and a wide range of possessions are defined as contraband.

Contraband includes things such as cash, chewing gum, some types of ink pens, some types of pencils, some types of clothing, some types of toilet articles, most jewelry, most metal, some types of reading material, all medicines, all illegal substances, weapons, and most decorations. In secure facilities, the personal possessions permitted an inmate are limited to a specific list. Anything not specifically permitted is prohibited. If personal shoes are permitted, they must be of an approved type and style. If personal toiletries are permitted, they must be of a specific brand, size, and style. If personal decorations are permitted in the living area, they are limited to size, type, and style.

Enforcement of the contraband rules is complicated by three factors. While the state provides all of the basic necessities including clothing, food, and toiletries, state provided supplies are basic at best and generally regarded as substandard by inmates. It is common for inmates to purchase some forms of clothing (shoes), food, and toiletries with funds provided by family members or from other personal resources. In most secure institutions personal items must be purchased from the institutional store. The institutional store intentionally stocks a very limited selection of items (usually one type of each item) to permit the easy identification of contraband. In institutions that permit visitors to bring items with them or permit family members to send Christmas packages, the items sent must conform closely to the items available in the store. The point is, personal items are often encouraged to reduce institutional operating costs and to reduce the impact of status deprivation. Second, in most cases the rules regarding contraband are not strictly enforced. If an inmate is well adjusted and the variation is minor, officers will not take notice of the deviation from the rules if the inmate is complying with the spirit of the regulation. Third, if the environment is too restricted, the ability of the officers to control the population declines. Simple boredom and stimulus deprivation both produce poor adjustment as inmates become psychologically stressed. This stress expresses itself in the form of misbehavior and resistance to the efforts of the officers to maintain control of the institution.

As the security of the institution and the security classification of the inmate increases the freedom of movement permitted the inmate decreases. In secure institutions, inmates have freedom of movement only when it is specifically permitted. In segregation units, there is no freedom of movement. Even recreation and exercise is severely limited and controlled. In some units, inmates are permitted some freedom of movement within the common area of the unit. In some units, the inmates are permitted the freedom of limited movement within the secure perimeter of the institutions. In all institutions some inmates (traditionally called trustees presently classified minimum out) are permitted limited freedom of movement outside of the perimeter of the institution. Typically inmates can only leave their assigned areas under supervision, with a pass, or at specific limited times. Limits on movement function to limit the ability of the inmates to exercise control over their environment which correctional employees believe that the inmates would use to compromise the integrity of the institution. Issues regarding freedom of movement are related both to preventing escapes and to the control of contraband. The issue in freedom of religion cases is frequently a freedom of movement issue. That is, should the inmates be able to meet as a group and control the activities in which they will engage and control the extent to which they will be supervised by correctional staff.

The disciplinary process is controlled by correctional employees. As is the case in most social settings, most control is informal. Officers control a number of resources and privileges in the inmates' environment. By judicious use of access to these resources and privileges, the officers reward and punish inmates for their behavior. In most cases, the officers are effective in maintaining control of the areas for which they are responsible without resorting to the use of the formal disciplinary system. If an inmate cannot be controlled through the use of these informal techniques, the officer writes a formal complaint. Minor complaints may be reviewed by an employee such as a caseworker. If the offender accepts the disposition imposed by the reviewer, no further action is taken. If the inmate rejects the disposition of the reviewer or if the offense is considered major, the complaint is reviewed by a disciplinary committee. The disciplinary committee is usually composed of security supervisors. In more relaxed institutions, the disciplinary committee may include representatives from industry, education, or classification to provide a more balanced review. If the offender rejects the disposition of the committee he or she can appeal the decision up the administrative line to the warden.

Development of the Issue

Inmate control and discipline issues have focused on due process in disciplinary matters, censoring mail, restricting reading materials, and standards for conducting searches in the correctional environment. Most of these issues emerged early in the history of prisoner rights actions (see Chapter 1).

Prison staff have complete control of the disciplinary process in all prisons. While the issue of grievous loss has been introduced into the deliberations, it is possible that degree of power exercised by the disciplinary committee is substantial. Removal of privileges considered minor by those outside the prison is substantial in the stark environment of the prison. These committees could increase the length of time the offender spent in prison by changing his security classification thus reducing the rate at which he or she earned good time and could remove accumulated good time or restore previously forfeited good time. While not challenged on this basis, the disciplinary committee, an administrative body, made decisions generally reserved for the court, a judicial body.

Prior to litigation, due process did not exist in disciplinary hearings. Most hearings were a perfunctory ratification of the decisions of the complaining officers. Inmates were not routinely notified of the specific nature of the charges nor permitted to present evidence in their defense. At times the offender was not present during the proceedings. The first decision that provided inmates some degree of due process rights involved the loss of good time (*Wolfe v. McDonnell*, 1974). This decision, based on a "liberty" right, give inmates the right to limited due process when severe disciplinary penalties could be imposed (Alpert & Hawkins, 1989). These limited due process rights had to be weighted against the valid state interest in maintaining control of the institution. The *Wolfe* decision was modified by subsequent decisions and was extended to some transfers to other institutions. In a collateral development, most correctional systems have developed formal grievance systems to provide due process for inmate complaints about prison conditions or actions of correctional employees (Carlson & Garrett, 1999).

Reading material is restricted. Inmates can only receive publications authorized by the administration. Correctional personnel seek to exclude reading material that is illegal and reading material that might foster rebellion and unrest in the prison. As with other areas, written material that is not specifically approved is disapproved. Generally speaking, pornographic material and material expressing political views endorsing civil disobedience, illegal behavior, or rebellion are disapproved. The volume of news and interest literature flowing into correctional facilities has been greatly expanded since the courts first ruled that inmates retained some of their rights.

Mail, telephone use, and visits have always been restricted on the theory that these activities facilitate both the flow of contraband into the institution and the planning of escapes. While mail, telephone use, and visitors can still be restricted and mail and visits restricted for disciplinary reasons, censorship and the ability to correspond with a reasonable number of friends and family members has improved. Correctional staff can limit the amount of mail or number of correspondents for reasons as simple as insufficient staff to properly process the volume of mail (Allen & Simonsen, 1998). Generally speaking, absent a compelling state interest, correctional staff cannot prohibit correspondence, calls, and visits indefinitely. They can restrict one or two of these activities but cannot isolate the inmate from the community (Carlson & Garrett, 1999). As is the case in the regulation of other rights, restriction of these rights must be reasonably related to legitimate state interests (Carlson & Garrett, 1999). Correspondence with counsel cannot be restricted and any censorship must be related to a clear state interest (Champion, 1990).

The courts have been less willing to restrict the ability of correctional staff from searching inmates when and where they choose. The compelling interest of the state is the control of contraband, particularly weapons and materials from which weapons can be made. Living areas are routinely searched and inmates are routinely searched as they move from one area to another, when they complete a visit, or when they return to the institution following an absence of any type. Searches are conducted at random irregular places and times so that inmates cannot identify patterns which would allow them to move contraband with reduced risk. While a few decisions have restricted searches if they are used to discriminate, to harass, or if the nature of the search can reasonably be expected to traumatize, for the most part, the right to search the inmate and his or her living area is unrestricted (Carlson & Garrett, 1999). While correctional staff cannot wantonly destroy inmate personal property, they can search visitors and correctional staff. These searches, however, cannot be unreasonably thorough. Generally, body cavity searches of visitors or staff must be based on probable cause (Champion, 1990).

Legal Decisions

Aside from *Wolfe*, mentioned earlier, the U.S. Supreme Court has rendered several decisions over the last three decades that have had a dramatic impact on inmate discipline and control behind the walls. In general, there has a been a definite swing from what some would term as overprotection of inmates' rights to a present status of minimum protection and a broad increase in discretion for correctional administrators in the operation of institutions.

The decisions in this area of the law beginning in 1974 with the *Wolfe* Court have focused on various aspects of confinement. There are, however, three pivotal decisions that are especially noteworthy regarding the standard by which administrative oversight and control of inmates will be limited.

First, *Turner v. Safley* was borne out of a class action lawsuit brought by inmates of the Missouri Division of Corrections challenging restrictions on inmate mail and inmate marriage regulations. The Supreme Court definitively held that where an inmate's constitutional rights are adversely affected by an institutional regulation, the regulation will not be invalidated as long as the regulation has a reasonable relationship to a legitimate penological interest. While prior decisions had seemed to establish this rule, *Turner* made clear the applicable standard. In accessing whether a reasonable relationship exists, courts are to look to see that the policy is not arbitrary and is applied in a non-biased manner.

Second, *Hudson v. McMillian* challenged as cruel and unusual punishment a beating Hudson suffered at the hands of Louisiana prison guards. Justice O'Connor, writing for the Court, held that excessive physical force used against an inmate may constitute cruel and unusual punishment even if the inmate does not sustain serious injury. O'Connor reaffirmed the standard as set forth in *Whitley v. Albers*, another excessive force case: force inflicted on an inmate violates the Constitution if the force is unnecessary and wanton.

Third, in *Sandin v. Conner*, the Supreme Court addressed the issue of disciplinary segregation as a form of punishment for nonconforming inmate behavior. In this case, Conner, a habitual offender, claimed that he was deprived of procedural due process when a prison disciplinary committee did not allow him to present witnesses at a misconduct hearing where he was sentenced to segregation for the misconduct. Conner filed a § 1983 claim. The U.S. District Court granted the prison officials' motion for summary judgment. But, the Ninth Circuit Court of Appeals held that Conner had a protected liberty interest in remaining free from disciplinary segregation. Relying on *Wolfe*, the appeals court held that Conner was denied procedural due process in the hearing because he was denied the ability to present witness on his behalf.

The Supreme Court reversed the Ninth Circuit, holding that the due process protections set out in *Wolfe* did not extend to internal disciplinary procedures. Chief Justice Rehnquist, writing for the Court, noted that the due process protections announced in *Wolfe* only apply to unlawful restraint relating to the original sentence imposed on the inmate. To invoke the protections of due process, the action of the prison officials must equal an "atypical [and] significant deprivation" of an inmate's restraint as related to the original sentence. In this case, the prison's disciplinary procedure, while punitive, did not affect the length of Conner's sentence and was consistent with the range of permissible deprivations that flow from being incarcerated.

Summary

Control will continue to be an issue in the relationships among participants in the correctional process. Inmates will continue to attempt to exert as much control over their environment and security personnel will continue to retain as much control as possible over the inmate's environment. Staff responsible for programs that require or that work best when inmates have increased freedom of choice and motivation to participate in programs will continue to mediate the negotiations between security personnel and inmates. As changes come and go, inmates will file suits if the change restricts inmate freedom and if it appears that a complaint focusing on the change can be effectively brought forward.

References

Allen, H.E. (1998). *Corrections in America*. Englewood Cliffs, NJ: Prentice Hall.

Alpert, G.P., & Hawkins, R. (1989). *American prison systems: Punishment and justice*. Englewood Cliffs, NJ: Prentice Hall.

Carlson, P.M. & Garrett, J.S. (1999). *Prison and jail administration: Practice and theory*. Gaithersburg, MD: Aspen

Champion, D.J. (1990). *Corrections in the United States: A contemporary perspective*. Englewood Cliffs, NJ: Prentice Hall.

Cases

Hudson v. McMillian, 112 S. Ct. 995 (1992)

O'Sullivan v. Boerckel, 119 S. Ct. 1728 (1999)

Sandin v. Conner, 515 U.S. 472 (1995)

Turner v. Safley, 482 U.S. 78 (1987)

Whitley v. Albers, 475 U.S. 312 (1986)

Wolfe v. McDonnell, 418 U.S. 539 (1974)

Chapter 10

Involuntary Civil Commitment of Sex Offenders

A number of behaviors have become defined as more serious or subject to control by society than they were considered to be in the past. Of these, none have been more sensitive or subject to such high levels of increased enforcement than sexual offenses, particularly sexual offenses in which children are the victims. Justice agencies have increased the attention and resources devoted to reducing, controlling, and sanctioning sexual abuse of children. Legislation and the development of aggressive new policies to accomplish these goals have produced a substantial body of legal opinion some of which directly influence the housing and release of convicted sex offenders and their supervision in the community on probation or parole. The primary issue is the balance that should be maintained between protecting the rights of the individual and protecting the public from a foreseeable risk.

Historically, many of the behaviors that are subject to intense social control today were considered to be private rather than public matters. The family and social institutions, such as the church, were expected to protect women and children from unacceptable sexual aggression. Victims were held accountable for their victimization in many cases with relatively weak excuses from offenders and their families accepted as reasons for the matter to remain private. The shift from private to public concern has been relatively recent in the case of child sexual abuse. Child sexual abuse emerged as an identified public problem in the 1970s in the United States and was not mentioned in Department of Health and Social Security brochures in Britain until 1980. In both countries, the estimates of the incidence of child sexual abuse were relatively low (one in a million by the American Psychiatric Association in 1975) (LaFontaine, 1990).

In early western legal development, the law defined as criminal only acts of anal intercourse between men and intercourse with animals by either men or by women (Gegeroff, 1968). Rape was a property or civil offense with compensation to the male (husband or father) who was responsible for the victim (Brownmiller, 1975). In the Statutes of Westminister (1275) forcible rape of women and statutory rape of girls were criminalized (Pallone, 1990). Victimization of male children was addressed in the context of anal intercourse with any male. Variations from 1275 to the mid 1900s had to do with changes in the penalties assigned rather than in the types of acts prohibited as illustrated in a series of reforms promoted by Sir James Fitzjames Stephen which produced legislative reform in Canada in the late 1800s (Geigeroff, 1968). These acts prohibited sodomy or attempted sodomy with men or women, sex with animals, indecent exposure, rape, and statutory rape (girls under the age of 12).

Child sexual abuse did not exist as a separate concept before the Sixteenth Century (Badger, Green, Jones, & Hartmen, 1988). Life spans were short, living conditions were crowded, classifications or differences among childhood, adolescence, and adulthood did not exist, and child sexuality was denied. The first laws prohibiting some aspects of child abuse (1584, sodomy with boys; 1576, forcible rape of girls under the age of 10) began to appear in secular and ecclesiastical statutes and principles in England. The concept of incest was not prohibited in secular law before 1908. During the first two thirds of this century, child sexual abuse was defined as a minor problem, receiving little attention from the police (Badger, Green, Jones, & Hartman, 1988). In the 1970s, child sexual abuse began to be defined as a serious social problem with increased reporting, enforcement, and treatment.

By the 1990s, the stage was set for the emergence of aggressive statutes that emphasized protection of the public in the United States. It is these statues which are being challenged in the courts today.

Child sexual abuse is a classic example of the conflict between psychiatry or treatment and the law. Mental illness has traditionally been held to excuse the offender. That is if the offender is mentally ill, he or she is not responsible for his or her behavior and the behavior is a symptom of mental illness, not a crime. Sexual offenders are either evil or mentally ill. If evil, they should be processed through the criminal justice system. If they are mentally ill, they should be processed though the civil mental health system and treated (Blakey, 1996). In the past, the debate centered on the criteria that should be used to determine if the offender is mentally ill or criminal. Recent legislation is challenging this dichotomy and creating a new class, guilty and mentally ill (Pallone, 1990).

Offenders whose offense behavior is limited to sexual offenses without accompanying non-sexual felonies are termed sexual psychopaths or habitual sexual offenders. The first sexual psychopath statues were enacted in the 1930s and tended to be modeled after the defective delinquent statutes of Massachusetts (1911) and Pennsylvania (1933) (Pallone, 1990). While these statutes varied considerably one from the other, most specified a compulsive predisposition or irresistible impulse to commit prohibited sexual acts and most specified treatment through involuntary detention until the patient was cured. Non-sexual psychopath sex offenders were considered ordinary criminals and sentenced to probation or prison with parole following normal processes for all criminal offenders. These statutes were most common in the 1960s and are still in force in many states, but they declined in the 1970s and 1980s as legislatures repealed the acts, in some cases replacing them with more restrictive acts that provide for indefinite civil commitments in lieu of criminal prosecution (Cornwell, 1996). During the 1980s, sexual predators increasingly were treated and processed as criminals rather than as mentally ill patients. During the 1990s dangerous sexual offender statutes added civil commitments to criminal sentences to extend the length of time the offender could be incapacitated, in many cases for the rest of his or her life (Francis, 1995). These statutes should capture dangerous mentally ill offenders, thus, if the offender is dangerous but not mentally ill, he or she should not be detained (Zanini, 1997).

The most recent acts in this area focus on sexual predators who have been prosecuted and processed as criminal offenders who are nearing the end of the sentence imposed as a result of their criminal conviction. In essence, the offender is treated as both a criminal and a mentally ill person. The criminal process satisfies the need for a penalty. When the penalty has been executed and is nearing completion, the offender is processed as a mentally ill patient and civilly detained for treatment.

Recent Decisions

During its 1996-97 term, the U.S. Supreme Court decided that the civil commitment of sex offenders for treatment after they serve their sentence of incarceration is constitutionally permissible. At issue in *Kansas v. Hendricks* (1997) was the Sexually Violent Predator Act of 1994 which provided a procedure for the civil commitment of sex offenders who, because of "mental abnormality" or "personality disorder," were likely to recidivate once released from prison.

Leroy Hendricks was a repeat child molester and deviant whose career dated to 1955 with a conviction of indecent exposure. Two years later, he was convicted of lewdness with a young girl and served a two-year jail term. In 1960, he was convicted of molesting two boys and drew a two-year sentence for those offenses. While on parole for those offenses, he was convicted of molesting another young girl. After treatment as a sexual deviant in a state hospital, Hendricks was deemed safe for release and discharged from treatment in 1965. In 1967, he was convicted of two other counts of molesting a child, and, after refusing to par-

ticipate in a treatment, served a five year term. A declared pe-
dophile, Hendricks sexually abused his stepchildren for approximately four years after his 1972 release. His next conviction came
in 1984 for molesting two young boys; the sentence he was serving for those offenses formed the basis for this case.

Hendricks challenged the constitutionality of the Sexually Violent Predator Act, alleging that the Act violated substantive due
process principles, that the Act amounted to an ex post facto law,
and that enforcement of the Act violated the Double Jeopardy
provision of the Fifth Amendment of the U.S. Constitution. The
Kansas Supreme Court struck down the Act on substantive due
process grounds, finding that the Act's "mental abnormality" requirement was not sufficient to meet the standard of "mental illness," as required for involuntary civil commitment. The Kansas
court did not address Hendrick's ex post facto and double jeopardy claims.

The Sexually Violent
Predator Act (SVPA)

The SVPA was enacted after the Kansas Legislature found evidence that the civil commitment procedures in place at the time
were inadequate to address the problem of sex offenders who did
not suffer from a mental disease or other defect sufficient to invoke the then present procedures (Kan. Stat. Ann. § 59-29a01
(1994)). Further, the Legislature determined that the probability
of rehabilitation for sex offenders in prison was poor and that
long-term treatment was necessary for these individuals. As a result, the Legislature established the civil commitment procedure
at issue, aimed at the long-term care of sexually violent predators
after their release from incarceration.

Under the Act, a sexually violent predator is "any person who
has been convicted of or charged with a sexually violent offense
and who suffers from a mental abnormality or personality disorder which makes the person likely to engage in... predatory acts

of sexual violence" (Kan. Stat. Ann. §59-29a02(a) (1994)). A "mental abnormality" under the SVPA is "a congenital or acquired condition affecting the emotional or volitional capacity which predisposes the person to commit sexually violent offenses in a degree constituting such a person as a menace to the health and safety of others" (Kan. Stat. Ann. §59-29a02(b) (1994)).

Under the SVPA, the custodial authority is required to give 60 days notice to the prosecuting attorney of the anticipated release of the convicted sex offender. The prosecuting agency then has 45 days to determine whether to petition the court for the involuntary commitment of the individual. A probable cause standard served as the court's guide in its determination as to whether or not the felon was a sexually violent predator under the SVPA. If the court found that the individual met the statutory requirements of a sexually violent predator, then the individual was transferred to a secure facility for evaluation. After the evaluation, a trial was held to determine whether the individual was a sexually violent predator. If the individual is adjudged a sexually violent predator, then the individual is transferred to a state facility for treatment until the disorder is sufficiently checked so that the individual can safely return to everyday society.

In addition to the strict procedural process, other safeguards were in place to insure that the individual's procedural due process rights were observed. For offenders subject to the SVPA who were indigent, the state was required to provide medical evaluation by mental health personnel. Additionally, indigents were provided counsel for the proceedings and were afforded the opportunity to call witnesses on their behalf, cross-examine state witnesses, and review real evidence presented by the state.

The Act Satisfies Substantive Due Process Requirements

The U.S. Supreme Court reversed the Kansas Supreme Court's finding that the Act violated substantive due process principles.

Justice Thomas, writing for the Court, noted our history of strong support for freedom from physical restraint; however, this freedom from restraint is not absolute. Accordingly, the involuntary civil commitment of a specific subgroup of known dangerous persons (i.e. sexual predators) is entirely consistent with the traditional concepts of freedom.

Individual Liberty versus Public Safety

As early as 1905, the Supreme Court acknowledged in *Jacobson v. Massachusetts* that absolute liberty must bow to greater concerns for public good. In *Jacobson*, the defendant was arrested and detained for violating a mandatory smallpox vaccination order by the Cambridge Board of Health. In sustaining the mandatory vaccinations, the Court established that:

> [t]here is ... a sphere within which the individual may assert the supremacy of his own will , and rightly dispute the authority of any human government, especially of any free government existing under a written constitution, to interfere with the exercise of that will. But, it is equally true that in every well-ordered society charged with the duty of conserving the safety of its members the rights of the individual in respect of his liberty may at times, under pressures of great dangers, be subjected to such restraint, to be enforced by reasonable regulations, as the safety of the general public may demand. (*Jacobson v. Massachusetts* 197 U.S. at 29)

Justice Thomas further made it clear that Kansas' SVPA is substantively and procedurally sound from a due process perspective. The procedure requires a showing of actual dangerousness. Further, the commitment proceedings only trigger for those individuals who have previous convictions for sexually deviant behavior. The state must demonstrate not only that the subject is a convicted sex offender but that his present mental state is indicative of repeat behavior in the future. As Justice Kennedy noted in *Heller v. Doe* (1993), "[p]revious instances of violent behavior are an important indicator of future violent tendencies" (*Heller,* 509 U.S. at 324).

Of course, a showing of a sexually predatory past could not, alone, be sufficient to sustain involuntary commitment, but past acts coupled with a present mental abnormality, illness, or the like will suffice. The SVPA meets this requirement, by requiring a finding of a sexually predatory past, future dangerousness, and a present mental abnormality or other similar illness.

Mental Illness and Mental Abnormality

Hendricks strongly urged the Court that the SVPA did not comply with the Court's earlier decision in a Louisiana case. In that case, *Foucha v. Louisiana* (1992), the Court overruled the state's practice of confining an individual with an antisocial personality after his acquittal of criminal responsibility for insanity and his service of a period of time in a mental health facility. The Court had previously held in *Jones v. U.S.* (1983) that it is unconstitutional to hold an individual acquitted for insanity in a mental health facility for a period extending beyond a time when he ceases to be a danger to himself or society. Additionally, the Court had decided that it was unconstitutional to institutionalize a harmless mentally ill individual after the basis for the initial commitment ceased to exist (*O'Connor v. Donaldson,* 1975).

In *Hendricks,* the Court did not accept the argument that the statutory language of "mental abnormality" was not equivalent to the "mental illness" language referred to by the Court in *Foucha.* Mental health professionals regularly disagree on exactly what is meant by mental illness. Further, the Court itself has used various terms in cases involving mental illness to describe the conditions. Thus, the terminology differences cited by Hendricks were not of significance to the majority. Justice O'Connor has noted that the state is justified in committing an individual as long there is a medical reason for the commitment (*Foucha v. Louisiana*, 1992).

Double Jeopardy/Ex Post Facto Not Implicated by SVPA

Hendricks unsuccessfully argued that the SVPA established a criminal proceeding and as such effectively amounted to his being forced to answer twice for the same offense. The Court observed that legislative intent is key in determining whether a statute was intended to be civil or criminal in nature. Where a legislature defined the nature of the statute, then deference is paid to the legislative statement. In this case, the state's placement of the SVPA in the Kansas Probate Code instead of the Kansas Criminal Code and the statute's stated purpose of creating a civil proceeding lends credence to the state's argument that no criminal sanction was intended. While statutory labels are not dispositive of a statute's effect, as long its effect is not so punitive as to clearly defeat any proposed or stated civil purpose, then it will be deemed civil in substance and effect (*U.S. v. Ward*, 1980).

Additionally, the Court noted that the SVPA did not impose retribution in that it did not require a previous conviction for its imposition and there is no intent requirement for the SVPA to operate. Additionally, the statute did not seek to deter violent sexual acts because persons suffering from mental abnormalities are unlikely to be deterred by the threat of confinement. Also, the period of treatment is tied to the correction of the mental abnormality that triggered the initial confinement. Once the abnormality is under control, the individual will be released. Finally, the commitment period is reviewable annually and if the state chooses to confine individuals for more than a year, they must again prove that the individual abnormality is still effecting the behavior. Similarly, Hendrick's ex post facto argument was rejected by the plurality because the SVPA is not punitive in its operation.

Treatment... For Now

The SVPA was upheld by a slim majority of the Court—5-4. The crucial fifth vote came from Justice Kennedy, whose vote turned on the ex post facto issue. Kennedy is weary of using a civil commitment statute in concert with the criminal code. He noted the civil intention of the statute, but cautioned that the practical effect of the statute could be lifetime confinement. Kennedy clearly indicates that in his mind this issue is not closed. Should there arise a situation in which civil commitment statutes were to become a tool for states to impose retribution or if the aim is general deterrence, then such statutes may fail. Similarly, if it were shown that the state's label of mental abnormality does not offer a firm foundation for concluding that the civil commitment is warranted, then he does not feel that Court precedent in this area would support such statutes.

The Dissent: The SVPA Amounts to an Ex Post Facto Law

The dissent, written by Justice Breyer, supported the majority's conclusion that the definition of "mental abnormality" provided for in the SVPA satisfied substantive due process standards. The dissent found fault in the fact that the state, while arguing that the confinement was for treatment, failed to provide Hendricks with treatment while he was serving his criminal sentence. Further, the dissent believed that the SVPA violated ex post facto principles as applied to Hendricks. While the SVPA purported to treat Hendricks for his mental abnormality, the Act's effect was to inflict further punishment on Hendricks. The very claim by the state that the Act is for treatment and the triggering mechanism of the labeled statute causes operation only after completion of a incarceration period gives the SVPA an inescapable punitive character. Justice Breyer found troubling the fact that evaluation for the treatment program was delayed until the near end of the individual's criminal confinement term. This provided evidence that treatment of the individual was not the treatment of the predator. Additionally, the state had not provided funding for the treatment program for Hendricks and others similarly situated.

In short, the dissent found fault with the SVPA only as it applied to Hendricks. The SVPA, or similar statutes, which operate prospectively are constitutionally sound. Where the aim of such statutes are clearly treatment, retroactive application would be appropriate; however, in this case, the primary stated purpose of the SVPA was not treatment but further punishment.

Summary

Legislation often follows public will, particularly in the area of criminal law. When public anger becomes aroused by a specific type of offender, control of that offender becomes a priority for the criminal justice system. The role of the appellate system in these cases is to assure that the legislature, in its desire to satisfy the voting public, does not trample the personal rights of the offender. Child sexual offenders cause intense concern because children are so vulnerable and case histories tend to identify child sex offenders as highly likely to repeat their offenses on release. Because they are perceived as exceptionally dangerous, greater restriction of their rights can be tolerated, including life-time commitment for treatment.

Clearly, statutes whose aims are to offer legitimate treatment for mentally ill sex offenders upon their release from a punitive sentence are constitutional. Not one member of the Supreme Court suggested that such statutes per se, were unconstitutional; however, the fact that a state attaches a "civil" label to a statute does not make it civil in operation or effect. The stated purpose of the statute must be shown in its operation. While in this case the statute was upheld, civil libertarians need not overly concern themselves with similar statutes. At best, there exists a four vote core for such statutes. It seems that the crucial issue is whether the commitment statutes function as ex post facto laws—that is, are they punitive in operation and do they come after the end of the original sentence. State legislative bodies should proceed with caution in drafting such legislation and ensure that future statutes similar in nature to the SVPA do not run afoul of ex post facto prohibitions.

References

Badger, L.W., Green, N.A., Jones, L.R., & Hartman, J.A. (1988) *Child abuse in the deep south*. Tuscaloosa, AL: University of Alabama Press.

Blakey, K.P. (1996). The indefinite civil commitment of dangerous sex offenders is an appropriate legal compromise between "mad" and "bad"—A study of Minnesota's sexual psychopathic personality stature. *Nortre Dame Journal of Law, Ethics, and Public Policy, 10*, 227-256.

Brownmiller, S. (1975). *Against our will: Men, women, and rape.* New York: Simon and Schuster.

Cornwell, K. (1996). 1293 protection and treatment: The permissible civil detention of sexual predators. *Washington and Lee Law Review, 53*, 1293-1307.

Francis, S.H. (1995). Sexually dangerous person statutes: Constitutional protections society and the mentally ill or emotionally-driven punishment? *Suffolk University Law Review, 29*, 125-135.

Geigeroff, A.K. (1968). *Sexual deviations in the criminal law.* Toronto, Canada: University of Toronto Press.

LaFontaine, J.L. (1990). *Child sexual abuse.* Cambridge, UK: Polity Press

Mayer, A. (1988). *Child sexual abuse.* Homes Beach, FL: Learning Publications, Inc.

Pallone, N.J. (1990). *Rehabilitating criminal sexual psychopaths.*
New Brunswich, CT: Transaction Publishers.

Sexually Violent Predator Act, Kan. Stat. Ann. § 59-29a01 et
seq. (1994).

Zanini, P. (1997).Considering Hendricks v. Kansas for Massachusetts: Can the constitutionally detain dangerous persons
who are not mentally ill? *New England Journal on Criminal
and Civil Confinement, 23,* 427-436.

Cases

Foucha v. Louisiana, 504 U.S. 71 (1992)

Heller v. Doe, 509 U.S. 312 (1993)

Jacobson v. Massachusetts, 197 U.S. 11 (1905)

Jones v. U.S., 463 U.S. 354 (1983)

Kansas v. Hendricks, 117 S. Ct. 2072 (s1997)

O'Connor v. Donaldson, 422 U.S. 563 (1975)

U.S. v. Ward, 448 U.S. 242 (1980)

Chapter 11

Looking to
the Future

There is a well-established history of inmate driven litigation, much of which has always been directed toward challenging their convictions or the length and nature of their sentences. Substantial inmate driven litigation directed toward challenging the conditions of the plaintiff's confinement has been occurring for less than 50 years. In the early days, following the successful breach of the hands-off doctrine, the flood of litigation flowed from the prisons to the courts unchecked. In the intervening years, both corrections and court staff have learned how to manage the flow so that much of the frivolous litigation has been discouraged or is handled in summary fashion. Even so, the flow of legal documents from the prison to the courts is still substantial and is likely to remain so for the near future.

Reducing Frivolous Complaints

Correctional staff have worked to reduce the flow of complaints to the court by developing alternative avenues for complaints and by reducing some of the benefits of filing legal complaints. Most departments of corrections now manage functional grievance systems. Inmates with complaints can receive a legitimate hearing on any complaint. The courts now require inmates to exhaust internal mechanisms for grievances before turning to the courts. In some cases, the inmate is satisfied with the process;

in others, the department of corrections builds a substantial record of the circumstances of the complaint and staff efforts to equitably resolve the complaint. This record bolsters the state's case in court. In the process, many frivolous complaints are dropped. A second initiative also discourages frivolous complaints. Some departments of corrections have built courtrooms within one or more of the prisons in the system. Federal judges have cooperated with these efforts to discourage litigation. Frivolous complaints can be quickly processed and the inmates loose the trip to town that frivolous complaints produced before the courtrooms were constructed. While these two initiatives reduce frivolous complaints fairly effectively, legitimate complaints continue to flow to the courts.

Conservative Trends

U.S. society appears to be at the peak of a punishment and retribution cycle. Prosecutors, judges, and legislators appear to believe that a necessary and possibly sufficient element in electability is conservative sentencing. In this environment, legislators pass increasingly restrictive and punitive statutes; prosecutors push cases in which the transgression is minor or the transgressor is not a serious offender to conviction with recommendations for severe sentences, and judges impose the severe sanctions the new laws allow in many cases.

This conservatism is reflected in the Supreme Court. As justices leave the court, they are replaced by more conservative justices. These justices generally act to reduce the liberties of offenders and expand the rights of victims and justice system officials. It is likely that the court will continue in this tradition until public sentiment changes and new justices appointed to the court favor a more liberal perspective. The cycling of justice system philosophy endorsed by the public has swung from extreme liberal to extreme conservative with some degree of regularity.

Punishment and retribution as the appropriate disposition of convicted offenders is dominant at the present. The present preference for punishment developed in the 1970s and has influenced legislation, policy, and practice. Legislation enhancing habitual offender statues, providing for determinate sentencing, restricting the ability of departments of corrections from housing some offenders in some types of housing, and providing longer sentences when specific conditions are present have increased the number of offenders sentenced to prison, provided for longer sentences, and made prisons more difficult to administer. The practical consequences of these actions have been to produce overcrowded prisons and to reduce the ability to use punishment to control offenders.

Punishment tends to become dominant when treatment is perceived as ineffective in curing offenders, crime is perceived as increasing, and the risk of the public to criminal victimization is seen as increasing. Punishment is perceived to have a deterrent effect, and long incarceration is perceived to have an incapacitation effect. It is anticipated that the combination of deterrence effect and incapacitation effect will reduce victimization by reducing crime.

The ability to sentence severe offenders to prison and to maintain them for long periods of time is effectively prevented by overcrowding which is caused by implementation of the various sentencing reform statutes. Prisons were overcrowded when the shift from treatment to punishment began.

A series of judicial decisions in the 1960s established minimal standards for humane living conditions that continued to be reinforced into the seventies. A central position in many of these decisions addressed population density, forcing many prison systems to reduce the number of inmates housed in existing facilities thus defining many operating prisons as overcrowded. In many cases, court orders prevented, and in some cases still prevent, exceeding specific population limits for specific jails, correctional facilities, and correctional systems. While more recent decisions have modified the earlier rulings, upper population limits are in place for many correctional institutions.

As the problems develop, secondary adaptations that avoid one of the statutory provisions emerge. For example, the court might not take judicial notice of the presence of three prior felony convictions when sentencing a specific offender thus avoiding the mandatory prison sentence or the need to enhance the sentence appropriate for the offense. Pressure to use incarceration remains, producing an uneasy balance in the sentencing process which causes some less severe offenders to be incarcerated while more severe offenders are released. When added to the process that causes some more severe offenders to be released rather than some less severe offenders, the degree of risk to which society is exposed increases rather than decreases.

Statues with mandatory sentence enhancement and mandatory life without parole provisions are vulnerable to court challenge. The mandatory provision in many of these statutes has been included to answer criticism that such acts are discriminatory. If the imposition of a sentence is automatically applied to a set of circumstances related to the offense, it is not discriminatory. The decision to avoid taking judicial notice of conditions requiring the application of a mandatory sanction effectively removes the direct link between the conditions relative to the crime and the sentence.

At some point, it is probable that the application of these statues will be challenged as discriminatory. It is probable that in the near future there will be a shift in philosophy from a preference for punishment in the disposition of offenders to a preference for treatment as a disposition for criminal offenders. It will be held that punishment is expensive and does not work. As a result a situation in which public sentiment for treatment will develop, producing a new wave of treatment-oriented reform.

As the new liberal cycle matures, pressure will be created for reform. Prosecutors, judges, and legislators will believe that a liberal position on justice is a necessary and potentially sufficient element for electability. Legislative initiatives will change, prosecution patterns will change, and sentencing patterns will change. Justices appointed to the Supreme Court will be more liberal and the inevitable challenges will produce litigation. In the near future, however, litigation will continue to reflect resistance to a conservative ideology.

Consent Decrees

Consent degrees were a product of a liberal environment. During the 1960s, prisons, county jails, and city jails were under attack by proponents of inmate rights. While the focus appeared to be on the state departments of corrections, inmate advocacy groups were active in every state. In many cases, the process was not as adversarial as it appeared to be. Correctional administrators covertly supported the actions of these groups, at times, writing the briefs for the inmate complainants. Correctional professionals preferred to improve the facilities they managed and successful suits allowed them to leverage state legislatures, county commissions, and city commissions into providing adequate financial support. Many of the suits that were brought were settled by consent decrees. That is, the defendants (correctional staff) agreed to make specific and, at times, detailed changes and the plaintiffs agreed to drop the suit. Some of these decisions were never appealed beyond the federal district court and have been held to have the status of settled principle.

Recently, these consent decrees have come under challenge. In some cases, such as Alabama, the state returns to federal court and asserts that federal supervision is no longer needed because the state department of corrections is now substantially in compliance with constitutional standards. In other cases, the legitimacy of the original consent decrees is challenged. It is likely that this trend will continue in the near future.

Trends in Litigation

Access to the Courts, Libraries, and Legal Assistance

The right of inmates to have access to the courts to air their grievances is almost certain to be preserved in the foreseeable future. The courts appear to be attempting to develop a standard, which will allow legitimate complaints to move forward while frivolous complaints are addressed and diverted in the institutions themselves. It is fairly likely that as departments of correction refine the programs to process complaints internally, complaints about the legitimacy of the process and complaints that raise legitimate issues regarding the rights of inmates in institutions will continue to be brought forward. While the volume of complaints will have diminished greatly, cases will continue to be brought forward on a regular basis.

Impact of the Prison Litigation Reform Act

The Prison Reform Litigation Act was specifically designed to reduce the increasing flow of frivolous cases to the federal courts. It has been upheld as a legitimate restriction on the rights of inmates and will reduce the number of cases that are heard by the courts and will reduce the impact of favorable decisions on the operations of correctional facilities. While there will probably be further challenges to the act itself, it is unlikely to be greatly restricted. It may also create a condition of increased litigation on the part of correctional officials who can be expected to move to remove or reduce existing consent decrees that do no meet the stringent standards for consent decrees imposed by the act.

Impact of the Religious Freedom Restoration Act (RFRA)

It is likely that suits addressing restrictions of religious freedom will be few in number in the coming years. The right to practice one's religion regardless of incarceration is well established. The compelling public interest in both legislation and judicial decisions allows correctional authorities to protect themselves from unsafe and threatening practices.

Most departments of corrections have adopted supportive policies. That is, the practice of legitimate religion is promoted. Chaplains typically have broadened their skills to include the facilitation of a broad range of beliefs and work actively with any group of inmates who choose to become more religious by any legitimate standards. As departments of correction staff have shifted their orientation toward supporting all religious activities regardless of the type of religion, cases alleging denial of religious freedom are both likely to arise and will be more difficult to support when they are frivolous.

Impact of Sentencing Reform

Sentencing reform may produce the next wave of cases before the court. Challenges of specific sentencing strategies been largely unsuccessful. As a result, sentencing reforms such as sentencing enhancement statutes, habitual offender statues, and punitive sentencing statues for drug offenders are producing rapidly growing prison populations. The growth in the number of inmates held in prisons across the nation has and will continue to out strip the construction and commission of new prisons. Existing prisons are becoming overcrowded reproducing many of the deteriorating physical conditions that served as the basis for many of the successful suits of the 1960s.

While the present Supreme Court is more conservative than the court that overturned the hands-off doctrine, there will be a point at which the court will intercede based on the constitutional rights related to cruel and unusual punishment. Inmate advocates will recognize this potential and will file suits seeking redress for improperly detained inmates and reform of the systems.

Issues in the Incarceration of Death Row Inmates

Most death statues include provisions for automatic appeal of the sentence. While many states have streamlined the appellate process for capital cases, there will be a steady flow of cases through state and federal court systems as these appeals are pursued. Challenges have been raised regarding undue pain associated with executions. This issue has not been resolved and can be expected to produce continuing litigation. As the death row population increases in size producing overcrowding, litigation may emerge challenging the living conditions on death row.

Issues in Privatization

Privatization has a long history of controversy in corrections. Early in this century labor and management banded together to restrict the use of inmate labor to produce products for the open market. As a result, products produced with inmate labor are generally restricted to use by state agencies. While new programs such as work release and cooperative relationships between manufacturers and correctional administrations that involve the use of inmate labor in private enterprises are becoming more common, resistance from the private for profit community has not emerged. This most certainly is due to the care with which these programs avoid the appearance of unfair competition. Inmates are generally paid prevailing wages and usually accept jobs that are not attractive to "free world" labor.

The second face of privatization, the use of private for profit contracts to manage and administer correctional facilities or specific correctional services, is more likely to produce litigation in the future. As it has been held that § 1983 complaints (and by extension other complaints) cannot be avoided by shifting administrative responsibility to a private contractor, these cases will continue to come before the courts. It is also likely that suits challenging the transfer of inmates to out of state private facilities will emerge. Litigation can be expected in this area until the issues involved in the use of private contractors to deliver correctional services are resolved.

Standards of Medical Care

Correctional administrators have developed working practical systems to deliver effective medical services to inmates in almost all of the jails and prisons in the United States. Many of these administrators have chosen to place the delivery of medical services in the hands of private contractors, others have chosen to place the control of medical services and medical policy in the hands of medically trained personnel. As it is unlikely that correctional administrators will move away from a solution that is both more effective at delivering medical services and more cost effective, litigation in this area is likely to be limited.

Discipline and Inmate Control

Control will continue to be an issue in the relationships among participants in the correctional process. Inmates will continue to attempt to exert as much control over their environment and security personnel will continue to retain as much control as possible over the inmate's environment. Staff responsible for programs that require or that work best when inmates have increased freedom of choice and motivation to participate in programs will continue to mediate the negotiations between security personnel and inmates. As changes come and go, inmates will file suits if the change restricts inmate freedom and if it appears that a complaint focusing on the change can be effectively brought forward. Litigation on these issues can be expected to continue into the foreseeable future.

Notification and Continued Confinement of Sexual Offenders

When public anger is aroused and focused on a specific issue, legislators respond. Frequently these responses are extreme and at times poorly crafted. Both of these conditions provide fertile ground for litigation. The weaknesses of sexual offender notification and labeling statutes are beginning to be noted both in litigation and in legislative reform. Statutes that permit the incarceration of sexual offenders beyond the terms to which they have been sentenced will continue to be controversial and will continue to produce litigation. The pubic is still aroused regarding sexual offenders so additional restrictive litigation can be anticipated as can the inevitable legal challenges to the constitutionally of those statutes.

Summary

There has been a great deal of change in the manner in which our correctional institutions are managed since the 1950s. Much of this change has been driven by the decisions rendered by two liberal federal district judges and by the willingness of correctional administrators to use restrictive decisions to lever legislative and administrative bodies into providing the support needed to reform the correctional system which, at that time, was under attack by reform oriented activists. Those who resisted the pressure to reform tended to be overwhelmed by the social pressure for reform that was brought to bear.

Most of the fundamental issues raised were successfully addressed and today's inmates enjoy a range of constitutionally protected rights that were unheard of before the 1950s. Litigation continued even though the prison conditions that produced the reform were substantially corrected. Much of this litigation was frivolous and driven by the success of earlier "impossible" cases, a desire to challenge correctional officials, and collateral benefits such as trips to town when complaints were heard by the courts. The volume of cases before the court coupled with increasing conservatism and a corresponding punitive orientation toward inmates, produced a set of decisions and litigation designed to reduce inmate access to the courts and to limit some of the "freedoms" conveyed in earlier decisions.

Litigation will continue to be brought forward by inmates. Part of this litigation will be generated by inmate resistance to changes in the correctional environment and part will generated by continuing inmate efforts to increase the control they have over their environment. Of course, inmates are not the only litigants in the correctional environment. Inmate activists and citizens with an interest in the operations will also bring litigation forward. The only certainty is that litigation will continue.

References

Abadinsky, H. (1997) *Law and justice*. Chicago: Nelson Hall.

Abbott, C. (1995). Dam the RFRA at the prison pate: The religious freedom restoration act's impact on correctional litigation. *Montana Law Review, 56*, 325-347.

Allen, F.A. (1981). *The decline of the rehabilitative ideal: Penal policy and social purpose.* New Haven, CT: Yale University Press.

Allen, H.E., & Simonsen, C.E. (1998). *Corrections in America.* Upper Saddle River, NJ: Prentice Hall, Inc.

Alpert, G.P., & Hawkins, R. (1989). American prison systems: Punishment and justice. Englewood Cliffs, NJ: Prentice Hall.

Badger, L.W., Green, N.A., Jones, L.R., & Hartman, J.A. (1988) *Child abuse in the deep south.* Tuscaloosa, AL: University of Alabama Press.

Bates, S. (1937). *Prisons and beyond.* New York: MacMillan.

Blackmore, J., & Welsh, J. (1983). Selective incapacitation: Sentencing according to risk. *Crime and Delinquency, 29*(4), 505-527.

Blakeey, K.P. (1996). The indefinite civil commitment of dangerous sex offenders is an appropriate legal compromise between "mad" and "bad": A study of Minnesota's sexual psychopathic personality stature. *Nortre Dame Journal of Law, Ethics, and Public Policy, 10*, 227-256.

Bloom, I. (1998). Prisons, prisoners, and pine forests: Congress breaches the wall separating legislative from judicial power. *Arizona Law Review, 40*, 389-424.

Bowditch, C., & Everett, R.S. (1987). Private prisons: Problems within the solution. *Justice Quarterly, 4*, 441-453.

Brownmiller, S. (1975*). Against our will: Men, women, and rape.* New York: Simon and Schuster.

Butler, D. (1993). Cruel and unusual punishment takes one step forward, two steps back. *Denver University Law Review, 70*, 393-412.

Carlson, P.M. (1999) *Prison and jail administration: practice and theory.* Gaithersburg, MD: Aspen Publishers, Inc.

Champion, D.J. (1990). *Corrections in the United States.* Englewood Cliffs, NJ: Prentice Hall.

Chemerinsky, E. (1998). The Religious Freedom Restoration Act is a constitutional expansion of rights. *William and Mary Law Review, 39*, 601-636.

Cohn, A.W. (1987). The failure of correctional management: The potential for reversal. *Federal Probation, 51*, 3-7

Cornwell, K. (1996). 1293 protection and treatment: the permissible civil detention of sexual predators. *Washington and Lee Law Review, 53*, 1293-1307.

Costa, R.J. (1997). The Prison Litigation Reform Act of 1995: A legitimate attempt to curtail frivolous inmate lawsuits and end the alleged micro-management of state prisons or a violation of separation of powers? *Brooklyn Law Review, 63*, 319-366.

Cullen, F.T. (1986). The Privatization of treatment: Prison reform in the 1980s. *Federal Probation, 50*, 8-16.

Currie, E. (1985). *Confronting crime.* New York: Pantheon Books.

Decker, D. (1997). Consent decrees and the Prison Litigation Reform Act of 1995: Usurping judicial power or quelling judicial micro-management? *Wisconsin Law Review, 1997,* 1275-1321.

Deiter, R. (1996). *Twenty years of capital punishment: A reevaluation.* Washington, DC: Death Penalty Information Center.

Durham, A. M., III (1987). Correctional privatization and the justice model: The collision of justice and utility. *Journal of Comtemporaty Criminal Justice, 3,* 57-69.

Farris, L.S. (1998). Private jails in Oklahoma: An unconstitutional delegation of legislative authority. *Tulsa Law Journal, 33,* 959-977.

Flanagan, T. (1982). Correctional policy and the long-term prisoner. *Crime and Delinquency, 28*(1), 82-95.

Fogel, D. (1978). *We are the living proof, 2nd ed.* Cincinnati, OH: Anderson Press.

Francis, S.H. (1995). Sexually dangerous person statutes: Constitutional protections of society and the mentally ill or emotionally-driven punishment? *Suffolk Univeristy Law Review, 29,* 125-135.

Gandy, J. & Hurl, L. (1987). Private sector involvement in prison industries: Options and issues. *London Journal of Criminology, 229*(2), 185-204.

Geigeroff, A.K. (1968). *Sexual deviations in the criminal law.* Toronto, Canada: University of Toronto Press.

Gobert, J.L., & Cohen, N.P. (1981). *Rights of prisoners.* Colorado Sprigs, CO: McGraw-Hill.

Gold, M.E. (1996). The privatization of prisons. *The Urban Lawyer, 28,* 359-389.

Hawkins, R., & Alpert, G.P. (1989). *American prison systems: Punishment and justice.* Englewood Cliffs, NJ: Prentice Hall.

Henak, R.P. (1982). *Prisoners' rights. An annual survey of American law.* Dobbs Ferry, NY: Ocean Publications.

Hinckley, S.D. (1987). Bounds and beyond: A need to reevaluate the right of prisoner access to the courts. *University of Richmond Law Review, 22,* 19-49.

Inciardi, J. (1986). *Criminal justice.* New York: Harcourt Brace, Jovanovich.

Irwin, D. (1981). Sociological studies of the impact of long-term confinement. In D. Ward & K.F. Schoen (Eds.) *Confinement in maximum custody.* Lexington, MA: Lexington Books.

Janus, M. (1985). Selective incapacitation: Have we tried it? Does it work? *Journal of Criminal Justice, 3,* 117-129.

Jengeleski, J.I., (1986). Corrections; A move to privatization. In B.I. Wolford and P. Lawrenz, (Eds). *Issues in correctional training and casework.* College Park, MD: American Correctional Association.

Krantz, S. (1983). *Corrections and prisoners' rights.* St. Paul, MN: West Publishing.

Kuzinski, E.J. (1998). The end of the prison law firm? Frivolous inmate litigation, judicial oversight, and the Prison Litigation Reform Act of 1995. *Rutgers Law Journal, 29,* 361-399.

LaFontaine, J.L. (1990). *Child sexual abuse.* Cambridge, UK: Polity Press

Laycock, D., & Thomas, O.S. (1994). Interpreting the Religious Freedom Restoration Act. *Texas Law Review, 73,* 209-245.

Logan, C.H. (1987). The propriety of proprietary prisons. *Federal Probation, 51,* 35-40.

Lombroso, C. (1968). *Crime its causes and remedies.* Montclair, NJ: Patterson Smith (originally published in 1911).

Luttrell, M. (1990). The impact of the Sentencing Reform Act on prison management. *Federal Probation, 55* (4), 54-57.

MacKenzie, D.L., Tracy, G.S., & Williams G. (1988). Incarceration rates and demographic change hypothesis. *Journal of Criminal Justice, 16*(3), 212-253.

Maestro, M. (1973). *Cesare Beccaria and the origins of penal reform.* Philadelphia: Temple University Press.

Maltz, M. (1984). *Recidivism.* Orlando, FL: Academic Press, Inc.

Mayer, A. (1988). *Child sexual abuse.* Homes Beach, FL: Learning Publications, Inc.

McKelvey, B. (1977). American prisons: *A history of good intentions.* Montclair, NJ: Patterson Smith Publishing Company.

Milovanovic, D., & Thomas, J. (1989). Overcoming the absurd: Prisoner litigation as primitive rebellion. *International Journal of the Sociology of Law, 16,* 455-475.

Mohs, D. (1993). Opening and closing the door to Eighth Amendment excessive force claims. *Saint Louis University Law Journal, 37,* 489-498.

Montick, D. (1983). Challenging cruel and unusual conditions of prison confinement: Refining the totality of conditions approach. *Howard Law Review, 26,* 227-266.

Morgan, E.F. & Sigler, R.T. (1998). Sentencing into the twenty-first century: Sentence enhancement and life-without-parole. In Roslyn Muraskin (Ed.) *Visions for change: crime and justice in the twenty-first century,* (351-366)(rev.ed.). Singing River, NJ: Prentice Hall.

Murton, T., & Hyams, J. (1969). *Accomplices to the crime.* New York: Grove Press.

Pallone, N.J. (1990). *Rehabilitating criminal sexual psychopaths.* New Brunswick, CT: Transaction Publishers.

Palmer, J. (1991). *Constitutional rights of prisoners.* Cincinnati: Anderson.

Pelliccotti, J.M. (1987). 42 U.S.C. Sec. 1983 & correctional official's liability: A look to the new century. *Journal of Contemporary Criminal Justice, 3,* 1-9.

Rachanow, S.S. (1998). The effect of *O'lone v. Estate of Shabazz* on the free exercise of rights of prisoners. *Journal of Church and State, 40,* 125-149.

Rafaloff, J. (1988). The armed career criminal act: Sentence enhancement or new offense? *Fordham Law Review, 56,* 1085-1099.

Ratliff, W.L. (1997). The due process failure of America's prison privatization statutes. *Seton Hall Legislative Journal, 21,* 371-424.

Religious Freedom Restoration Act of 1993, Pub. L. No. 103-141, 107 Stat. 1488, 1993.

Robbins, I.P. (1987). Privatization of corrections: Defining the issues. *Vanderbilt Law Review, 40,* 813-828.

Savas, E.S. (1987). Privatization and prisons. *Vanderbilt Law Review, 40,* 889-899.

Sexually Violent Predator Act, Kan. Stat. Ann. § 59-29a01 et seq. (1994).

Shinnar, E., & Shinnar, K. (1975). The effects of the criminal justice system on the control of crime: A qualitative approach. *Law and Society Review, 23*(4), 547.

Silvester, D.B. (1990). Ethics and privatization in criminal justice: Does education have a role to play? *Journal of Criminal Justice, 18,* 65-70.

Smith, C.E. (1987). Examining the boundaries of Bounds: Prison law libraries and access to the courts. *Howard Law Journal, 30,* 27-34.

Solove, D.J. (1996). Faith profaned: The Religious Freedom Restoration Act and religion in prisons. *Yale Law Journal, 106,* 459-491.

Rudovsky, D., Bronstein, A.J., Koran, E.I., & Cade, J. (1988). *The rights of prisoners: The basic ACLU guide to prisoner's rights.* Carbondale, IL: Southern Illinois University Press.

Samaha, J. (1988). *Criminal justice.* Saint Paul, MN: West.

Smith, C.E. (1987). Examining the Boundaries of Bounds: Prison Law Libraries and Access to the Courts. *Howard Law Journal, 30,* 27-44.

Smollo, R. (1984). Prison overcrowding and the courts: A road map for the 1980's. *University of Illinois Law Review, 1984,* 399-421.

U.S. Department of Justice (1983). *Setting prison terms*. Washington, DC: Bureau of Justice Statistics.

Wilkins, Jr., W., Newton, P., & Steer, J. (1993). Competing sentencing policies in a "war on drugs" era. *Wake Forest Law Review, 28,* 305-327.

Wolfgang, M., Figlio, M., & Sellin, T. (1972). *Delinquency in a birth cohort.* Chicago: University of Chicago Press.

Zanini, P. (1997). Considering Hendricks v Kansas for Massachusetts: Can the state constitutionally detain dangerous persons who are not mentally ill? *New England Journal on Criminal and Civil Confinement, 23,* 427-436.